D0566375

BATIK UNLIMITED

BATIK UNLIMITED

BY JOANIFER GIBBS

PHOTOGRAPHS BY TOM B. BURGHER II

WATSON-GUPTILL PUBLICATIONS, NEW YORK

PITMAN PUBLISHING, LONDON

*To my beloved Guru-Deva, Meher Baba, and all realized ones
embodying the unity of divine truth everywhere.*

OM SHANTI

Copyright © by Watson-Guptill Publications

First published 1974 in the United States and Canada by Watson-Guptill Publications,
a division of Billboard Publications, Inc.,
One Astor Plaza, New York, N.Y. 10036

Published simultaneously in Great Britain by Sir Isaac Pitman & Sons Ltd.,
39 Parker Street, Kingsway, London WC2B 5PB
ISBN 0-273-00802-1

Manufactured in U.S.A.

Library of Congress Cataloging in Publication Data
Gibbs, Joanifer, 1947-
  Batik unlimited.
  1. Batik. I. Title.
TP930.G52 1974   746.6   73-21552
ISBN 0-8230-0460-0

First Printing, 1974

Acknowledgments

I'd like to express my deep appreciation and heartfelt thanks to the many people who were instrumental in the publication of this book: to Lenore Flushner, who first conceived the idea of a batik book, to Donald Holden for his wonderful guidance, and to the editors who worked with me, Diane Hines and Jennifer Place. A most sincere "thank you" must also go to Tom B. Burgher II for his expert photography.

I am also indebted to Sister Kathlene Feeley, President of Notre Dame College, for launching me into creative writing back in high school days, and to all the art instructors who have fired creativity all along the way.

I want to thank all the artists who were kind enough to contribute their work, and Walter F. Herman, Thomas G. Taylor, Chuck Klompus, and Richard Dudrow for their undivided assistance.

No acknowledgement would be complete without mentioning the steadfast support and encouragement that my Mother has given me throughout the years. She always had confidence even when I didn't.

Lastly I want to mention the untimely contribution of Richard Falkenstein, organic gardener and meditation guide at Koinonia. His deep spiritual insight has opened many doors, one of which being the peace of mind so badly needed to see this book through to its conclusion.

CONTENTS

Javanese Women Batiking. In Java, it's customary for women to do the waxing while the dyeing is done mainly by the men. Photo by L.A. Driessen, Hengelo. Courtesy of Ciba Review, *Switzerland*.

INTRODUCTION

Batik is the ancient art of "wax-resist" dyeing. The foundation for this process was laid thousands of years ago when man first noticed that wax and water don't mix. Ever since, artists and craftsmen the world over have been experimenting with ways to best utilize the potential of that wonderful discovery.

Most people associate "batik" exclusively with fabric decoration, but this really isn't the case. Aside from cloth, practically any substance that will accept wax and dye can be batiked.

Another misconception is that a batik must have the distinguishing veinlike dye lines, or "crackle," in order to be an authentic, honest-to-goodness batik. This just isn't true. Naturally, many artists do rely on crackle to enhance a batik's depth and color. Others, however, may not care for veining and refuse to let it command their compositions. So if you see a wall hanging without "crackle" and someone says, "that's a batik," they may well be correct. Whatever the artist decides to do is strictly a matter of personal taste.

In this book you'll not only explore the "traditional" age-old way to batik, but you'll investigate many other aspects of this medium that may be new to you and hence exciting.

To batik in the traditional fashion, you always follow the same procedure. First, you apply hot liquid wax to your cloth. (This acts as a mask, protecting the underlying surface of the cloth from the dye.) Next you immerse the cloth in a dye bath, dry it, and remove the wax. If different color combinations or more complicated designs are desired, the process is repeated on different sections of the cloth until just the "right" effect is achieved.

Before I go further, I've heard the word "batik" mispronounced so many times that I want to set the record straight once and for all. It's *baa* (as in the sound a lamb makes) and *teek* (as in "teak" wood). The term itself is an Indonesian word, appropriately meaning, "wax-writing." No one knows exactly where or when batik came into existence. The theory is that its origins must be Eastern, and this is supported by archeologists who have found swatches of batik cloth in tomb excavations from Eastern countries.

India, Persia, China, and Japan are most noted for their batiks. Although Africa is a bit removed from the East, it too has its share of treasures. Today, India is the last stronghold for this art, ranking Number One as the world's richest source of consistently unique batiks. Not only now, but in the past, certain Indian regions used rice starch to lengthen the life of their clothes. This thick paste, derived from rice grain, was the forerunner of batik wax resist.

Javanese batik is the best known. These craftsmen developed a high degree of proficiency through centuries of dedicated effort. To this day, Java has produced some of the most prized and intricately detailed batiks imaginable.

Indonesian Batik (*Above*).
Here is a typical batik using a repeated motif of floral sprays in shades of blues, brown, and white. Note the intricate lines and dots made with the tjanting. Courtesy of the Textile Museum, Washington, D.C.

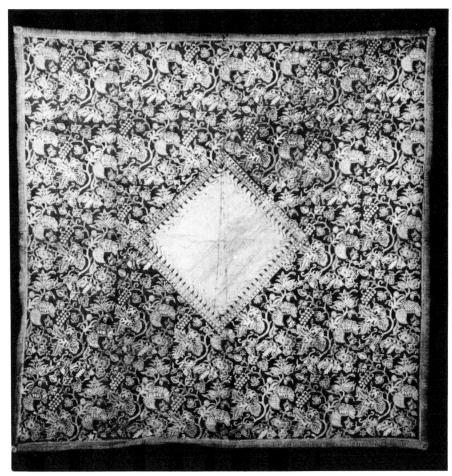

Javanese Batik. *This traditional headcloth shows a grape and vine motif. The colors are blue, dark red, and white overlaid with gold. Courtesy of the Textile Museum, Washington, D.C.*

All Oriental cultures have a great love for nature. This closeness and deep unity with the world of nature is expressed by the beautiful flora and fauna motifs present on their garments. Some of the designs are stylized, while others appear to be spontaneously created. Often they closely cover an entire span of cloth, giving an impression of gentle control and balanced grace.

When looking at one of these masterpieces it's hard to believe that the time-consuming traditional batik process was used. Unfortunately, these technical works of art often discourage the beginner. It is hard to conceive of the time and patience, much less the skill, needed to obtain such quality.

The incredible thing about Javenese work is that its high quality hasn't diminished from the time of its birth. Most art forms fluctuate, going through stages of mediocrity or genius. Yet in Java, as in so many parts of the East, time has stood still. We find we're left today with nothing but beauty, scarcely touched by technology.

In the 17th century, batiks were imported to Holland by Dutch traders traveling from the East. With their arrival, all of Europe soon knew about the process, but for some reason, Scandanavia was the only place where it thrived.

Eventually batik spread across the seas to America. Here, around the turn of the century, it was taken up seriously by some Art Nouveau fans, but never before has it enjoyed its present popularity.

The reason for this is twofold. Partly it's due to the shortening of the communications gap around the world. With the advent of television, everyone can now watch Indians waxing batiks on jungle floors, or priests, adorned in batiked robes, performing sacred rites. Quite often this type of viewing is our first meeting with batik.

The second reason for batik's expansive renaissance is the rebellion against mechanization. We have all come to realize the true value of hand-wrought goods. There's nothing special about an object that's been duplicated by the millions on assembly lines. But when one or only several of a kind exist, its value, both monetary and esthetic, soars.

Today crafts are flourishing. Everyone wants to be an individual, to stand out from the crowd and express the creative urge within them. I hope this book can help you to accomplish this.

As you become familiar with the basic "traditional" process, you might want to branch out and experiment with the other techniques for making a batik that we'll discuss. Trying out each new process will enrich your knowledge of a fascinating art. At the same time, you'll be able to decide if you have a favorite procedure you'd like to adopt, or if you'd prefer to combine techniques. In other words, the possibilities are as unlimited as your imagination.

Don't be surprised if your first efforts aren't Javanese museum pieces. You should see the first ones I did! With a little work and a lot of enthusiasm, your efforts will be rewarded, not only by the gratification you'll get from executing this art, but by the admiring looks your friends will give your creations!

Using the Tjanting. *Here a Javanese woman is placing the same wax design on the reverse side of the cloth. Courtesy of the Enoch Pratt Free Library, Baltimore, Maryland.*

1
TRADITIONAL MATERIALS AND TOOLS

Today, in areas of the Far East, people still approach many aspects of batik as they did centuries ago. Many still make dyes by hand from the natural vegetation of the countryside; others even weave their own fibers for the cloth they'll use. But these practices are becoming more the exception than the rule.

Few readers will have time to get *this* involved with dyes and fibers. However, for the ambitious, there are books devoted to the natural way of making your own dyes and fabrics (see Bibliography).

In this chapter you'll find out about the traditional Indonesian tools and methods for batik. You'll also find out exactly what equipment you'll need to begin batiking.

What Is Batik?

The whole batik process revolves around the principle that wax and water repel each other. When hot liquid wax is applied to cloth it hardens almost immediately. It then acts essentially as a mask, protecting that area of cloth from becoming saturated with water.

To illustrate this principle, paint a thin coat of rubber cement on a portion of a sheet of paper. Wait a minute for it to dry. Then paint tempera, acrylic, or any other water-soluble medium over the whole sheet. When the paint dries, briskly rub off the rubber cement with a paper towel or with your fingers.

What has happened? The original color of the paper has been retained in the area where the rubber cement was rubbed off. The rubber cement has thus "resisted" the paint.

In batik, wax works the same way. Dye cannot penetrate a fabric where wax was painted. These masked areas will retain the original color of the fabric, thus a design is formed when the wax is removed.

Traditional Tools

Tjanting tools and tjaps are Eastern implements traditionally used for applying wax to fabric. A tjanting is a metal cup with a spout; this cup is attached to a handle. Wax is held in the cup, much as ink is held in a pen. By tipping the spout slightly forward, wax will flow onto the work area. Minute details as well as bold lines can be achieved by using spouts of different sizes. With a tjanting you'll also obtain a distinctive line delineation that no other tool can quite duplicate.

The tjap is a metal printing block invented by the Javanese. It works on the same principle as a wood or linoleum printing block. Designs are first molded in metal and later affixed to a wooden block. These metal designs form a raised surface that actually "prints" the wax. The block is dipped in hot wax and presses hard against fabric, leaving an impression of the wax on the fabric. When the fabric is dipped in dye, the color takes only in the areas not covered by the wax design. If skillfully done, this method insures a flawless reproduction of very intricate details.

Machine-Made Batik

Tjanting work is time-consuming when compared with that of the tjap. It might take days, weeks, or even months to complete a richly patterned batik, whereas a similarly intricate pattern can be executed in half the time with the tjap. That's why the tjap alone is suitable for mass production. In fact, it's indispensable whenever batik clothing is manufactured. Large amounts of yardage would literally cost a fortune to batik with a tjanting.

But now even tjaps are gradually being replaced by modern machinery. This does have its positive aspects, for now everyone can own what once was reserved for the elite.

Dyes have also been affected by progress; aniline and other commercial dyes are taking over where vegetable dyes once reigned. Fortunately, these new dyes are improvements—they are more color-fast and resistant to wear and tear.

With these developments, it's easy to see why original, one-of-a-kind works are more prized than mass-produced ones, although only an expert with a trained eye can really tell the difference between the two.

Advantages of Traditional Batik

Batik permits an enormous amount of spontaneity and freedom of expression. With it, you'll get a fluid line that no other medium offers. Startlingly beautiful color combinations may suddenly appear when one color is dyed over another. One dyeing can produce two or more colors, depending upon the color of the fabric and the color of the dye.

Aside from being a versatile medium, batik promises that each effort will have that hand-crafted, personal look. No two people apply wax in precisely the same way, nor do they handle color with the same intensity or create line with the same movement. Even if you wanted to duplicate a batik exactly, it wouldn't be possible. It's refreshing to know that the artist's name isn't even needed for a batik to be an original.

Limitations of Traditional Batik

When you're working with wax, you can't correct mistakes as easily as you can erase pencil lines from paper. The nature of the medium makes even small corrections difficult. However, don't despair. Careful preparation beforehand will help eliminate pitfalls, and in Chapter 2 you'll find out how to remedy mistakes should they arise.

The "traditional" method also takes time; there's no doubt about that. The time needed for the fabric to dry between dye baths is the greatest consideration. Of course, you can make a simple two-color batik in about an hour, but for a truly intricate work, you must devote more time to the job.

List of Equipment

Here is a list of what you'll need to start batiking. This may look long, but don't let it fool you. Most of these items you already have around your house, and if not, you can improvise. (Items marked with an asterisk are optional.)

Fabric

Batik wax (beeswax, microcrystalline wax)

Tjanting(s)

Brushes

Pencils

Saucepan

Thermometer (candy or cooking type)*

Stove burner (double-boiler, electric hot plate, nightlight)

Dyes

Fix*

Dye bucket (plastic tub, vat, bowl, enamel sink, or basin)

Electric hand iron

Old newspapers (paper towels or old terrycloth towels)

Apron (smock or old clothes)

Rubber gloves

Cleaning solvent*

Wooden frame (homemade or artist's canvas stretchers)*

Wax paper*

Thumbtacks (pushpins)*

Clothesline and clothespins*

Scissors

Ruler*

Carbon paper*

Tracing paper

Fabrics

Now that you know what to purchase, here's some detailed information about individual materials. First, there are dozens of fabrics on the market, but only certain ones lend themselves to batik. Practically every fabric under the sun can be found in either department stores, fabric shops, or at wholesale distributors.

Best Choice. Pick finely woven fabrics like muslin, poplin, linen, percale, batiste, or 100% cotton. These all have smooth surfaces that accept dye well. You might also try wool, velvet, burlap, and corduroy, but a fabric with a raised nap must be waxed carefully. Natural silks and satins produce amazingly bright, vibrant colors, but are rather expensive for the beginner.

Avoid. Stay away from all synthetics and materials that have been chemically treated to be drip-dry, no-iron, or crease-resistant; the chemicals used in treating these fabrics interfere with the dyeing process. Some dyes will work on synthetics, but read the directions on the dye packages carefully to avoid disappointing results. Most heavy coarse fabrics aren't recommended. They absorb more wax and dye, take longer to dry, and are costly. Velvet, however, is the exception to the rule and meticulous waxing will assure lovely results.

All fabrics should be washed in warm water and mild soap before batiking. This will get rid of any unwanted sizing, starch, or bleach that could interfere with the dye's penetration of the fibers. It will also pre-shrink the cloth, so it won't shrink drastically later. You can also add some water-softener to loosen the fibers, which will help them accept the dyes later on. If you choose to use a colored material (other than plain white), you must boil the fabric first to remove any excess color that might interfere with the batik dyes.

Wax

The "standard" wax made especially for batik is a combination of 40% beeswax and 60% paraffin. Batik wax can be purchased in some arts and crafts stores. Approximately $1.75 will give you a one-pound box. This is by far the simplest wax to work with, for it requires no mixing; it is already a mixture of just the right proportions of the two elements needed for batiking. The only exception is if you want a heavy crackle, in which case you add more paraffin (I'll explain this later).

A problem is that batik wax is hard to find. With batik's growing popularity, I've found that most suppliers simply don't stock enough to handle the demand.

Beeswax. This comes in one-pound packages and can be purchased at art supply stores—or your local bee farm may have some extra lying about.

It can be used with or without paraffin, depending on the type of crackle you want. I've found that the mixture of both substances has a better spreading consistency than just the beeswax alone. Beeswax by itself, however, will insure that no "crackle" will be present in your final batik. This is because beeswax is much too soft and pliant to crack even with rough handling.

This wax has a higher melting temperature than paraffin, so you'll have to allow a few extra minutes for it to melt. The only drawback is the price. In it's pure form it runs about $4.00 per pound—which is outlandish. Bee farms carry the unrefined type, which is usually cheaper, but the problem with this primitive stuff is that it contains pollen particles that clog up the tjanting's spout. You can resolve this with a small wad of cotton or cheesecloth. Place the cotton or cloth on top of the spout as you pour out the wax and it will act as a filter.

Microcrystalline Wax. This is the chemical industry's answer to beeswax. Actually it's the waste product from oil refineries in a hardened form. It acts in the

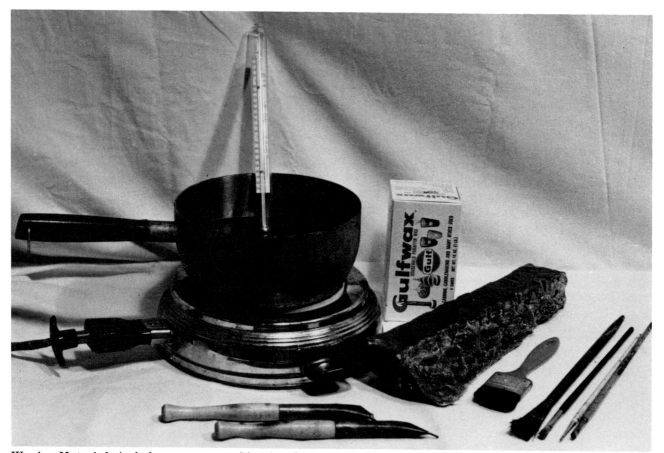

Waxing Materials *include a saucepan and heating element, wax, thermometer, tjantings, and brushes.*

same way beeswax does, having all of its properties. The great part is that it's less expensive!

It has been used for years by sculptors who were duplicating the lost wax process. Only recently has it been employed by batik enthusiasts, who usually use it in the same proportions as beeswax to paraffin.

It can be purchased at art supply stores in 10-pound slabs. If you plan on doing a fair amount of batik work, then this wax is for you. It's well worth the investment if you consider that batik wax is relatively expensive and pure beeswax is absurd, while you'll get a huge block of microcrystalline for about $5.00.

This substance comes in two distinct colors—light and dark. The dark variety shows up best on the cloth, and this helps you to see exactly where you've drawn your wax lines. If you remove this dark-colored wax by ironing, however, the heat of the iron will turn the cloth a light cream color in the areas that you've waxed. When the wax melts, it may spread and hit other areas that you meant to stay untouched. This color change won't be noticeable if you paint wax over the entire batik before de-waxing, or on a batik where all the colors are fairly dark or tonally subdued. It will only show up on pastel or rather lightly shaded cloth.

Paraffin. This wax substance comes in a one-pound box and is divided into four individual pieces for easy measurement and handling. It is available in most grocery stores, and some gas stations even carry it. A fairly common white household wax, it's used mainly for candle-making and canning purposes.

Paraffin is by far the most inexpensive wax, running a little over 25¢ for a whole pound. When it's mixed with any of the three waxes I've just described, it will add a crispness, a brittle quality, that causes the hardened wax mixture to break into tiny cracks when it's squished up in a ball. This gives the effect called "crackle" that happens when dye seeps into the cracks.

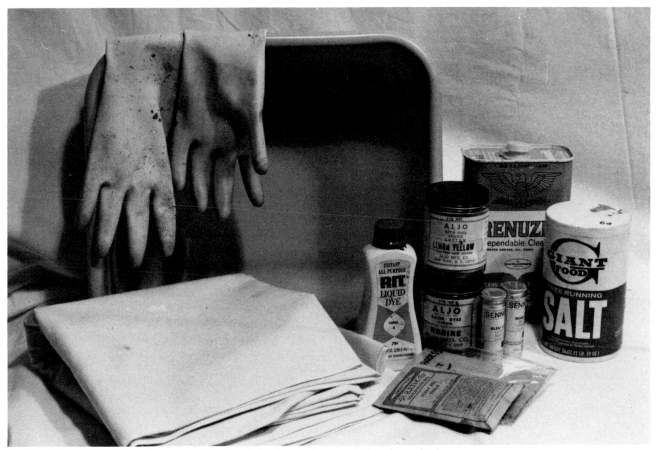

Dyeing Materials *shown here are cloth, dye tub, gloves, dyes, and cleaning solution.*

Tjanting Tool

This tool comes in three standard sizes: small, medium, and large. Most American models have only one separate spout, but tjantings can be imported with two or more, depending on what type of work you're doing. In Indonesia, there's even a tjanting called a *penado*, which has six spouts! Tjantings are sold in art stores, but you can make your own or have one made by a metal worksmith if you want a certain number of spouts.

Brushes

It's good to have a variety of brushes on hand for more versatility when you work. For instance, a large stiff-bristled 4″ brush (the type that house painters use) is ideal for tackling those large areas, especially if you're covering a whole surface with wax.

I suggest stiff bristles because they'll push the wax down directly into the cloth and not leave a thin residue on top, as flabbier brushes tend to do. For small details it doesn't matter if the bristles are stiff because the wax will soak into the fabric on its own if the wax is hot enough. A small-pointed brush will give a line much like a tjanting. Sizes ranging anywhere from ⅛″ to 4″ are handy to have.

There are various opinions about brush quality. Some people prefer using natural hair bristles of expensive camel, ox, or sable. These do last longer and won't become frayed and singed as quickly as the synthetic ones, but I personally prefer the less expensive kind. Let's fact it, once a brush has been dipped in wax, that's it. It just won't be the same again. Even if it's cleaned in solvents, it some-

Other Equipment *you'll need includes an iron, newspapers, items for securing your batik, and materials for transferring your designs.*

how never regains its former bounce. Any brush will perk up when returned to hot wax, but it should never be used for anything else once wax gets into its body and bristles.

This is why I use either tired old brushes, discarded from painting, or inexpensive hardware and dimestore ones. This way I don't get upset when they start to fall apart.

Pencils

Number 2b, soft lead is the best pencil I've found for drawing on cloth, as well as for making sketches on paper. Have several of these on hand before you start, so you won't have to keep jumping up to sharpen just one. Sharpening is needed more often when drawing on cloth because the lead tends to get used up much faster than when drawing on paper. A soft lead pencil slides across cloth with less pressure than the average medium to hard lead—it lets your ideas "flow" onto the material effortlessly.

Melting Equipment

Get a fairly large saucepan to allow the wax plenty of melting room so it won't run over the sides. This is especially true when you're melting down paraffin along with another type of wax, because there's more material to melt. Be sure it's an old beat-up pan—the wax sticks unless you wash it out well with a cleaning solvent.

Double-boiler. These are good to use if you want to be assured that the wax won't get too hot too quickly. Simply place a saucepan inside another larger pan or a frying pan (you can also use an electric skillet—the only method for heating, with the exception of an oven, that assures constant heat at a definite temperature). Put about ½ cup of water in the bottom of the large pan or the skillet. This method will prevent the wax from smoking heavily, but it will take a much longer time to melt down completely.

Thermometer. It's not necessary to have one, but you might find it helpful to check on the temperature of the wax from time to time. You can use either a candy or cooking type. Just attach it with wire to the side of the saucepan. Never touch it without using a pot holder—it gets mighty hot. Watch the red line and when it hits between 120° and 140° you'll know the wax is ready.

Electric Hot Plate. I frequently use a hot plate if a stove isn't available. The wax melts at about the same speed as on the stove. When using the stove burner, keep a close watch to check that the heat is not set at too high a temperature. Use a medium setting if you're working with an electric burner and a moderate to low flame for gas burners.

Nightlight. This is particularly good to use if children are batiking, in any classroom situation, or whenever a group of people are waxing at the same time. Merely remove the lid from a tin can—one that is broad at the top, so that another can will fit on top. Turn the can upside down and place it over the light (set the light into a holder to keep it upright). Punch some holes in the sides of the can to let air enter. Heat smaller tin cans filled with wax in a big saucepan or skillet, then transfer these to the top of the cans covering the nightlights. It's a lot safer for kids to work this way than directly over an open flame.

Dyes

So many brands of dye are available today that it's hard to make a choice. One thing to keep in mind is that if the fabric must be boiled right along with the dye solution, it's important *not* to choose dyes that require a high temperature to "fix" or secure the color. In other words, if the directions on the pack say to boil the dye *together* with the fabric to insure color-fast results, don't buy. It's fine to boil dyes. In fact boiling often helps some dyes to reach their most brilliant, true shades, but always remember to cool them before dyeing your fabric.

The reason for all this is that hot dye (above 110°) will melt the wax on contact, undoing all your efforts. Always read the directions, before purchasing, to be on the safe side. The best dyes to use are cold-water dyes, dyes that can be cooled after boiling, or dyes that use lukewarm water. Most dyes come in either powder or liquid form. It makes no difference which you use as long as the results are what you want.

After mixing the dye with water, add a mordant, or "fix." This is a substance that helps keep the fabric from later becoming discolored. One or two teaspoons of salt or vinegar stirred into the mixture should do the trick. Note, however, that aniline dyes already contain a mordant.

Rit and Tintex are commonly known dyes. You can purchase them in a grocery store or drugstore. Craftool, another popular brand, can only be found in art or craft shops. Alj carries the widest collection of colors as well as a good assortment of various types of dyes. Putnam, Dylon, Cushing, Fibrec, and Procion are also reliable brands. The suppliers list at the end of the book contains manufacturers you can write to for information on dye recipes as well as for lists of dye types and color variation assortments.

Re-Using Dyes. Some dyes can be saved and re-used, while others cannot. Whether or not a dye's strength will last through successive dye baths depends on its chemical content. You can never be certain as to how long a dye can be kept unless you experiment for yourself or write to the manufacturer.

One thing I *can* tell you from experience. If you open up a dye container after storing it for several weeks and happen to spot any mold, head to the nearest sink and dump it. The chemical reactions are dead and the mold has taken over.

You also might find that the dye has turned to a gelatin-like substance at the bottom of the dye jar. In advanced stages, the entire contents of dye solution may have turned into a pastelike mass. This, too, is annoying and also means that the dye should be thrown away.

Storing. When you find certain dyes that can be saved without loosing their strength, it's wise to save them in transparent plastic containers. This way you can see at a glance what color is inside without opening the top. It's also helpful to label them (using masking tape and a marking pen) with the name of the specific dye to avoid confusion. For instance, you might have a fuchsia and a rose bengal in separate containers. These two colors are so close in tone that unless they're marked you can't tell the difference between them.

Dye Bucket. Use either a plastic tub, vat, bowl, enamel sink, or basin. Any of these must be large enough to accommodate the entire fabric, so that it can slosh about freely and not be cramped. The amount of material to be dyed will help you choose which size to use. For six yards of fabric you would probably use a basement sink, whereas for a small piece a bucket will do. Dye tends to stain, especially sink enamel, so keep some strong cleanser nearby.

Electric Iron

An iron and newspapers are used to remove wax from fabrics. Ironing is only one of several ways to do this; you'll find out about the others later. Set the temperature of the iron according to the fabric you're using. If you're using a steam iron, don't fill it with water or use the steam-setting, because water might leak out and spot the cloth.

Cleaning Solvent

There are five main cleaning solvents: Clorox bleach, carbon tetrachloride, benzine, mineral spirits, and gasoline. They'll remove wax from fabrics, as well as clean off brushes and any other utensils that might be coated with wax. They all smell pretty bad and are highly inflammable.

Miscellaneous Materials

Here are some tools that may come in handy. They're nice to have in a pinch, but not absolutely required:

Wooden frame (homemade or painter's canvas stretchers). Elevates the cloth from the work table so that the wax won't stick.

Wax paper. Also keeps wax from sticking to the table top.

Thumbtacks (pushpins). Used to attach the cloth to the wooden frame.

Clothesline and clothespins. Used to hang up the drying material.

Scissors. Used to cut fabrics up into smaller sections.

Ruler. Employed for all fabric measurement.

Carbon paper. Used for transferring designs onto fabrics.

Tracing paper. With this, copies can be made of designs.

Old newspapers (paper towels or old terrycloth towels). The newspapers will catch wax that melts from the iron, protecting the ironing board, while the paper towels and cloth ones are for all general cleaning up.

Apron, smock, old clothes. Wear any one of these to keep those hard-to-remove waxes and dyes off of your good things.

Rubber gloves. These should be worn to protect your hands from harsh dyes and cleaning solvents.

Homage *by Joanifer, 6 x 6 feet. This batik captures a bit of ancient Egypt's glory. A vivid purple background contrasts the sun's brilliant yellow, and rose bengal crackle contributes a subtle glow.*

2

THE TRADITIONAL
BATIK PROCESS

This chapter will explore the entire traditional batiking process step-by-step. You will also see how this time-honored method of rendering design on fabric with wax forms the basis for other techniques discussed later in this book. Once you feel comfortable with this traditional process, variations of it will be easy.

Washing the Fabric

Wash your fabric carefully with soap and water. Boil the fabric if it's colored to remove any excess color that might interfere with the batik dyes. Hang the cloth to dry on a clothesline. When it's dry, iron out any wrinkles that may have formed because of the washing.

The Design

Decide what type of design you want. (The next chapter, "Ideas and Where to Find Them," will help you do this.) You might want to make some preliminary sketches on scrap paper before transferring the design to cloth (see Chapter 4). If you want controlled work, then this type of preparation is necessary. If you'd prefer a more uninhibited piece, then you can design as you go along, without preparation.

A good way to become acquainted with this medium is to try out a few small "practice" batiks. Get out your wax, tjanting, and brush and alternate between the brush and the tjanting trying out various lines to see the potentials of both implements. If your pieces are successful, you can mount them on cardboard and use them for greeting cards. But if these, hopefully "happy," surprises should turn into nightmares, you can toss them out without feeling that you've wasted valuable cloth. Old sheets are good to use for these first experiments; as you gain confidence, you can tackle a finer-quality fabric.

Positioning the Fabric

There are three ways to position the fabric. Try each one, and then decide which way works best for you.

Canvas Stretchers. Get some canvas stretchers at an art store. They come in various sizes, so choose the size that will give you the most service (small if you favor small batiks and large if you plan to do mostly bigger things).

You can make your own fabric frame from four pieces of lumber that they'll cut for you at a lumber yard. You nail these together at right angles to form your frame. The next step is to tack the material to the wooden foundation on all sides. Begin tacking in the center and work out toward the corners. As you tack each part, pull the cloth slightly to remove any wrinkles from the center. Never

The Traditional Process

Step 1. *Wash the fabric in a mild soapy solution and warm water. This can be done by hand or in the washing machine.*

Step 2. *Plan your design by making sketches, doodling, or looking through books. You might want to make a few practice pieces before starting a major work.*

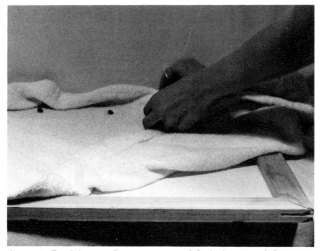

Step 3. *Position and secure your fabric in one of the ways described in this chapter. Here it's being tacked to a canvas stretcher.*

Step 4. *Unwrap the wax and put it in a medium-sized saucepan. Melt the wax at a medium temperature until the surface of the wax is lightly smoking.*

Breaking Up Wax. *Here a 10 pound slab of microcrystalline wax is being broken into smaller pieces prior to melting.*

Step 5. *Apply the melted wax to the fabric with a brush or a tjanting (shown here). A piece of cardboard is held underneath the tjanting to catch any stray drops of wax.*

The Waxed Fabric. *This photo shows the fabric after the waxing is finished.*

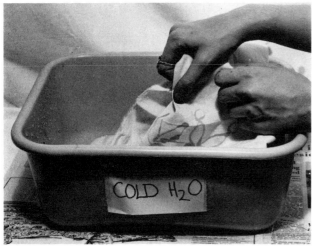

Step 6. *Crumple the waxed fabric while you're immersing it in cold water. This process will cause the wax to harden and crack so you will produce veinlike lines on your fabric when it is dyed.*

Step 7. *Combine your dye and water together according to package directions.*

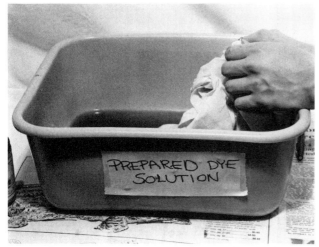

Step 8. *Submerge the fabric in the dye solution until the desired color has been reached.*

Step 9. *Remove the wax from the fabric by ironing over several layers of old newspapers. In the photo above you can see the melting wax being absorbed into the newspapers.*

pull too tightly or thin materials might rip. The great thing about a frame is that it not only holds the fabric in place, but it elevates the fabric so that wax won't stick to the underlying surface.

If the design you've drawn on the cloth, or planned out in your mind, extends beyond the area of the frame, take out the tacks and move the cloth around as you wax.

Wax Paper. When you're working with your small practice pieces, I suggest placing the fabric on top of a piece of wax paper instead of using a frame. This paper will catch any stray wax and save the time of tacking and retacking on a frame. Anyway, it's hard to find a frame to fit small pieces of cloth, unless you make it yourself.

You may find it easier to use the wax paper all the time, but be careful when picking up the material. When you pull it up, some of the wax could come off and leave parts of the material exposed. If this happens, you must retouch with wax before dyeing.

Clotheswasher, Clothesdryer, or Dishwasher. For large work, or if you're in a hurry, this method is for you. However, you must own either a clotheswasher, dryer, or dishwasher with a top, rather than front opening. These appliances have airtight lids that will clamp down hard on fabric and position it firmly.

Double up the cloth at one end to form a thickness that will hold, and place this beneath the lid, clamping down. The lid's heaviness will prevent the cloth from falling out. Now simply hold the fabric out over the floor and wax. Keep newspapers on the floor to catch any wax drops.

Preparing the Wax

When melting regular batik wax, simply drop the pound package into a saucepan (no mixing is required, as it already contains the right amount of paraffin).

If you're using either beeswax or microcrystalline wax add an equal amount of paraffin to each substance (one-pound to one-pound is the easiest ratio to use). The exception is if you want more "crackle" running through your batik—then add more paraffin.

All the other waxes come in easy-to-handle one-pound packages, except the microcrystalline. To my knowledge it always comes in the 10-pound slab, and so it must be broken up before it can be used. You'll have to break up the whole slab into separate sticks to start. You can do this all at once to get it over with or you can chip off one part at a time as needed.

Measure the sticks to insure that each one is equal, and draw lines to separate them with a felt-tip marker. Take a screwdriver with a wide head and place it along the edge of a line. (You may first want to run a knife blade heavily down each line, to make a ridge so the screwdriver will fit snugly.

Then, holding the screwdriver steady, whack the handle a few times with a hammer. Continue down the line until all parts of the line have been covered, and then try to break off a stick. If it's not loose enough by now, turn the block over and make duplicate lines on the other side, then repeat the process.

Melting the Wax

You can use any of the heating appliances discussed in the previous chapter. All work well and accomplish the same thing; it's a matter of preference.

For convenience, you might want to start out using a hot plate. While you're waiting for it to get good and hot, unwrap your wax and break it up (if necessary) into small pieces.

Here's a tip about melting wax. When all of your wax and paraffin is in hardened form (that is, when you first buy it) it will take longer to melt the first time you heat it. After having melted down once, it won't take as long to melt when you heat it a second time. Allow for this time element when working. As you probably know, wax can be used repeatedly. It never loses it's innate quality by getting stale, as dyes sometimes do.

The best temperature to use when waxing is between 120° and 140° F. You can tell when it has reached this temperature even without a thermometer, for the wax will smoke slightly and give off a pungent odor. After working around this smell for a long time, you may become light-headed, so it's best to have either an exhaust fan, an airconditioner, or a door or window open for direct ventilation. Otherwise the fumes are toxic and may give you a queezy stomach to boot.

Another thing to remember is that super-hot wax is extremely inflammable. You shouldn't leave the room for an extended period, or you'll be playing with fire—literally. Watch the wax constantly, so it won't get too hot. If it ever does ignite, don't panic, just place a lid quickly over the top or toss salt or baking soda on it. *Never use water* to douse or you'll need Smokey Bear!

Applying the Wax

Make sure the fabric is completely dry before you begin or the wax won't penetrate. Also make sure newspapers are underneath the area you plan to wax. If

Step 1. *First draw your design on the fabric, or use one of the methods of transferring a design discussed in Chapter 4. This design will use yellow and blue dyes.*

Step 2. *Wax all portions of the fabric that you want to stay white, or the original color of the fabric.*

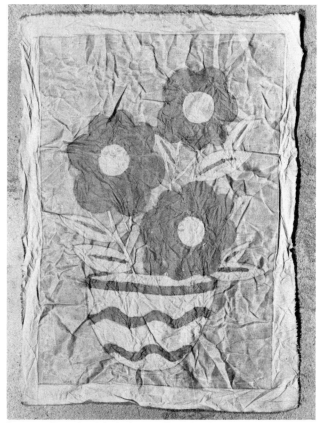

Step 3. *Dye the fabric in a yellow dye bath. This will color the areas that will be yellow and green. Then wax the areas that you want to stay yellow.*

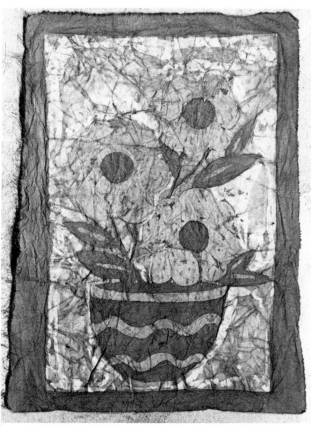

Step 4. *Now dye the fabric in a blue dye bath. This produces green when dyed over the exposed yellow areas. Wax the portions that should stay green.*

Step 5. *Redye blue, crumpling the fabric for veinlike lines, and you're finished with the dyeing process. Then just remove the wax by any of the methods discussed.*

wax does drip off the paper, you can scrape it off with a knife after it hardens. When moving a tjanting or brush from the wax pan to the fabric, hold a towel or a piece of cardboard underneath to catch stray droplets that might fall.

Using the Tjanting. Dip your tjanting far enough into the liquid wax solution to fill the reservoir, but not to overflowing. Then tip the tjanting forward so wax will flow freely onto the cloth. Be sure the wax is hot enough or it will clog up the spout. If this happens, heat the wax again until it smokes slightly. Return the tjanting to the mix and the obstructing wax will melt.

On the other hand, if the wax is too hot it will flow out too quickly from the spout and spread in all directions when it hits the fabric. This will cause details to blur and will also thin out the wax considerably. This thin wax won't resist the dye effectively. Don't get discouraged; the more you work with wax, the easier it will be to tell when the right flow and temperature have been reached.

A cardinal rule for waxing: to resist the dye, wax must penetrate straight through to the back of the material wherever it is applied. If the wax is hot enough, it will turn darker than its original shade and have a transparent quality when it hits the cloth. This means it has fully penetrated the fibers. Otherwise, it will be a yellowish white and appear opaque. This means it's only on the surface of the cloth. Turn the cloth over from time to time, to see if the reverse side is as dark and translucent as the front. If it isn't, then you'll have to wax the back.

Using Brushes. When using brushes, the same things that applied to the tjanting hold true. For waxing large areas, you can use a large brush and really fill the bristles full of wax. With details, though, you've got to be careful. Here, an overly charged brush would saturate and obscure fine lines.

Always run the tip of the brush along the side of the pan to get rid of excess droplets. Synthetic brushes will singe or fray if dipped into very hot wax. If this happens, remove the brush and cool the wax down. You can still use a battered brush for big spaces—I still have one that's been in service for three years.

Cooling and Crumpling

Now, before proceeding, you'll have to decide if you want your batik to have "crackle," the network of tiny, veinlike lines that appear when dye seeps through cracks in the wax. These cracks are made by letting the wax harden on the material and then crushing the fabric into a ball. The amount of paraffin added to the wax mixture will determine how brittle the wax will get. In other words, for more crackle add a larger amount of paraffin. Crackle often adds great beauty and pleasing textural unity to a composition. The choice, however, of "to crack or not to crack" is up to the individual craftsman.

The following may help you decide how you'll approach the problem of "crackle." Take a long look at your sketch—or think about your design or pictorial presentation. If it is so detailed that any cracks would interfere with its total delicacy, then forget the crackle. But if the picture is bold in concept or would be enriched by that Old-World flavor so treasured and revered by batik fanciers, then crumple that waxed fabric to your heart's content.

To make just a few cracks, your wax mixture should not have much paraffin, if any. Now let the fabric cool normally for about 10 minutes. Don't bunch or crumple it at all, especially when dyeing.

If you want lots of heavy veining, fold the cloth up and put it in the refrigerator for 5 to 10 minutes. For faster cooling, toss it into the freezer, but don't leave it in long; it will freeze hard in no time. On removal, crush the cloth with your hands and work it into a ball, moving it about vigorously.

If you want the crackle to follow a certain directional pattern, you can experiment by folding the fabric in a variety of ways to see which techniques to please you most.

You can also place crackle exactly where you want it after you've waxed. Instead of submerging the cloth in a dye bath, spread the fabric out on a hard surface and paint dye directly into the cracks with a brush. If you're going to dye the fabric again, wax over the areas you don't want to crackle further. This will protect them from dye action.

Preparing the Dye Bath

Follow the package directions to the letter, not forgetting to add the mordant. Many dyes already contain one, but it doesn't hurt to add another or more of the same. It will just help fix the color even more permanently.

You may strain the dye through a mesh strainer to filter out any solid bits of color that might have sunk to the bottom.

Dyeing the Fabric

Wet the fabric well, to get the fibers ready to accept the dye. Put on rubber gloves so your hands won't turn colors. Make sure the dye is lukewarm to cold before submerging the fabric, and remember that the fabric should be able to slosh about freely, unhampered by a small space. This will prevent streaking and uneven distribution of color. You should use enough dye solution to cover all portions of the fabric.

Fabrics should stay submerged in the dye anywhere from 10 to 45 minutes, depending on the depth of color desired. During this time, you should stir occasionally. If you don't want to wait a long time for a darker hue, then strengthen the mix by adding more concentrated dye. Keep in mind that wet, dyed cloth is always several shades darker then when it's dry. This is important to realize so you'll know when to remove the fabric.

It's a good idea to make some test strips first out of old sheets. Cut up a few small pieces and stick them into various dyes for different periods of time. When they're dry, make a note of which color was used, the amount of dye prepared, and the length of time it was kept in the pan. You might like to cut up your test swatches and attach them, along with the data, in a scrapbook for easy reference. Remember also that every color is affected by the succeeding ones that are dyed over it. (See the Putnam color chart on p.61)

Remove the fabric from the dye and rinse it well to remove excess color. If the color has become too dark, then keep rinsing for a few minutes and it will lighten gradually.

To dry, wring out any excess water and hang the fabric up on a clothesline. A plastic line is best; cotton ones often smear the dye. Use clothespins to hold the fabric at both ends. (Never hang over a line in the middle or an unsightly line will result.) When fabric is hung up to dry, all dye will eventually fall to the bottom. It's best to occasionally blot the bottom section with towels to prevent too deep a shade from forming there.

If you want extra fast drying, hang in front of a radiator or near an electric heater or an open oven. Turning up the house heat in winter also hastens drying. In summer, outdoor drying is best. An open line in the shade (out of direct sunlight) will insure the fastest drying imaginable.

Removing the Wax

After dyeing just one or all of your colors (you'll find out in a minute how to dye several colors), the batik is ready for wax removal. Here again you have options:

An Electric Iron. This is what I prefer to use. Remove the ironing-board cover so wax won't ruin it, and place a layer of newspapers (at least two weeks old) on the board. Old ones are best because fresh ones have a tendency to leave newsprint behind on the cloth. Then put the batik rightside up on top of these. Another layer of papers goes on top of the batik. By layer, I don't mean your whole Sunday paper. Just two or three sheets (or enough to cover) will do.

Set the iron at the setting required for the kind of fabric you're using. When

Zebras in Love. *This is an example of a traditional batik from South Africa made by an unknown artist. It is a simple batik done in only two colors.*

the iron is hot, move it firmly over the surface of the papers. After a minute or two, you'll notice that the papers are becoming coated with wax. When they're completely coated, change them—not just on top, but underneath too. Keep replacing with clean papers until all the wax has disappeared.

Solvents. You can use any of the ones I listed in Chapter 1. They all do the job and all smell equally as bad, unfortunately, so work with plenty of fresh air in the room. Just put the fabric in a bowl of solvent and slosh about well. Most of the wax will dissolve. Keep those rubber gloves on when sloshing, as these solvents are rough on skin.

Boiling Out Wax. You can boil out wax if the dyes are *completely* color-fast, as with chemical-reactive and cold-water dyes. Otherwise all or some of the color will boil away, leaving you with a washed-out mess.

Pop the fabric into a large pan of boiling water containing 1 tablespoon of detergent and 2 tablespoons of mordant. stir and wait for the wax to rise to the top. Then dump the fabric into cold water and repeat. When the wax floats to the top, you can scoop it up in a strainer and recycle it for your next project.

Never throw wax in any form (solid or liquid) down the sink, or severe stoppage may occur. The only thing that will solve this dilemma is a plumber or some Drain-o.

Scraping Off Wax. Place the cloth on a hard surface. Take an old kitchen knife with a fairly good blade, or a hardware tool like a paint scraper, and scrape away the wax. Don't do this too roughly, or you might tear through the cloth. This method only gets the surface wax, so you'll need to boil or iron out the rest later. You can, of course, salvage this wax too.

Dry-Cleaning. After each of the methods just listed, dry-cleaning is recommended. The exception is if the fabric is to hang freely from poles; you may wish to keep a little wax in the fabric to keep it just stiff enough to hang smoothly. Traces of wax also help repel dust and give a soft luminescence to your work. Dry-cleaning will also remove the stink of the solvent. If you plan to frame your finished work by stretching it on stretchers, you must dry-clean. Ironing or any other method is just not enough to totally remove all residue wax jrom the fibers. If, after stretching, there is any trace of wax present, the slightest temperature change will melt the wax and cause it to buckle no matter how tightly it was stretched; cold temperatures will similarly cause the fabric to contract. Although dry-cleaning is expensive for large amounts of yardage, it's still necessary; my advice is to use a coin-operated machine.

Don't resort to machine-washing unless you're positive that the dye you've used is *color-fast*. Even then, if it's an intricately detailed design that you prize highly, always dry-clean. You'd never think of throwing a rare piece of silk in the washing machine, or a woven piece of rich tapestry or embroidery; treat your batiks with the same respect.

Dyeing Two or More Colors

Now that you know about the basic one-color batik process, we'll go into dyeing more colors. It's best to start out by choosing a simple design and dyeing only one color on top of another.

You can use white or colored material to work on, but if the material's colored be sure that the shade's not too dark. If it is, then the color or colors you dye over it may not show up to their best advantage. After all, batik is a type of negative color process whereby colors are added, going from light to dark in sequential order. Try to think this way before dyeing each new shade.

If you want a colored cloth, then you can dye the overall piece yourself (for example, if you want a yellow fabric and your cloth is white). Just mix up the yellow dye, plop the fabric in, and wait for the dye to take. When it's dry, you can begin as you would for a one-color batik.

Wax all the areas you want to stay yellow and dye your second color, let's say red. After you iron out the wax you'll have a two-color batik—the yellow background and the red design.

Now let's do a more complicated dyeing job. For advanced dyeing processes, you'll always start out dyeing the lightest color first. It's helpful to work out your color scheme ahead of time, so you won't have problems (consult the Putnam color chart).

For your first dyeings, it's sometimes easiest to choose two colors closely related on the color wheel, so they'll enhance each other—for instance light blue and dark blue, or light brown and burnt sienna.

Procedure

If you want to dye three colors (not including the white background, which if counted makes four) here's what you do. The colors are yellow, green and blue.

1. Draw the design.

2. Wax all portions that you want to stay white.

3. Dye the parts to be yellow and green in a yellow dye bath.

4. Wax all areas that are to stay yellow.

5. Now dye blue. This produces green when dyed over the exposed yellow areas.

6. Wax the portions to stay green.

7. Redye blue. This will give you a blue-green effect (resulting from the overdyeing), but it will blend in well with the other colors after de-waxing.

Note: Always check before waxings to make sure that no wax has fallen off. If it has, rewax before dyeing, so the colors stay pure, or as pure as they can, for allover dyeing can't help but affect the underlying colors to some degree). Wax over the whole batik (even the areas which are now blue-green) if you want the color to remain solid and unaffected by the melting wax should you decide to use the iron-out method. This will use up more wax, but the results are worth the trouble.

Problems and Solutions

Here are some problems you're likely to encounter in batiking:

Sun Fading. I advise never to expose a batik to direct sunlight over an extended period. After a couple of years colors are bound to fade a little no matter how indelible the dyes are supposed to be.

Correcting Mistakes. If you want to change a line or color on your batik, use a cleaning solvent. Be sure the area to be changed is free of all wax. Then sponge or brush on a little solvent. Let it soak in, then repeat until the color has disappeared. Now you can wax or redye the area.

Emphasizing Important Areas. You may want to retouch certain spots after the final de-waxing. To do this, use thickened dyes or textile pigments (see Chapter 8). For example, you might want to brush over some black outlines if they look faded or washed out. Another brushload of the same color will give just the right highlight or accent. An iron's heat will set the added color.

Changing Dyed Colors. If you decide to change the color in some areas of your batik, you should first remove wax from these places. Then you bleach out the unwanted shade and redye. Instead of bleaching, you can also dye another color on top of the first one, provided it's dark enough to show up.

Clouds Fly By by Mari Eagerton. A flowing batik, both the clouds and the circles in the background create movement—they seem to float beyond the boundaries of the fabric.

3
IDEAS AND WHERE TO FIND THEM

If you're very observant, you'll find that potential ideas are everywhere just waiting to be tapped. You might be surprised to know that many people would love to be creative—to get deeply involved in an art or craft—but never do. Unfortunately most people stop before they get started, only because of a lack of ideas. Stop a minute to consider that a work of beauty is only a thought, plus a few hours of fun-filled work.

For batik, as well as for all other arts and crafts, two questions must be answered before you can get down to work: what type of thing should be made (a picture for a wall or a utilitarian object) and how should it be decorated (should the image be abstract or geometric, surrealistic or representational)?

While you're working, try to keep in mind that every line, form, space, color, and texture is vitally important to the total look of your batik. Each should work together to bring harmony and unity to the whole composition.

Observing Nature

One of the best direct sources of design inspiration is nature.

Take a trip to the zoo and look at the variety of animal patterns to be found: zebra and tiger stripes, panther spots, snake skins, and exotic bird plumage are just a few.

Go into your back yard or visit a park in the spring and watch the insects: look particularly at butterflies' wings and caterpillars' skins.

Look at the outsides of fruits and vegetables, then cut them open to see how the seeds are arranged. Cloud formations, sea shells, waves, and snowflakes are all exciting. Rocks, pebbles, cornhusks, pine cones, gourds, and dried flowers all offer inspiring design possibilities.

Other Sources

Aside from nature, there are many other idea avenues open to the inquistive artist. Here's a list of some that I've found invaluable:

Design books. Consider both primitive and contemporary designs.

Art history books. Look at books on both the past and present.

Biology books. These contain fascinating photos of micro-organisms.

Library picture files. Most large central branches carry complete picture files on every subject under the sun.

Magazine and newspaper clippings. Keep a scrapbook or file of these, labeled by category for easy reference.

Fruits and Vegetables *offer exciting design possibilities.*

Natural Objects
*not only provide
design ideas but are
easily obtainable.*

Scribbling *is not only fun, but can often result in surprising creative ideas.*

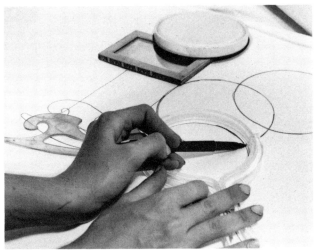

Outlining *objects found around the house can produce interesting results.*

A Viewer *will give your vision new perspective. Make one by cutting a 1″ x 2″ rectangle from a piece of cardboard.*

Sponging *with either a natural or synthetic sponge dipped in paint will produce various patterns depending on the amount of paint used and the pressure of the sponge.*

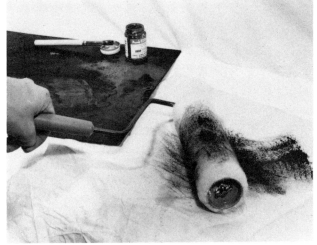

A Paint Roller *coated with thickened dye can make interesting patterns directly on the fabric.*

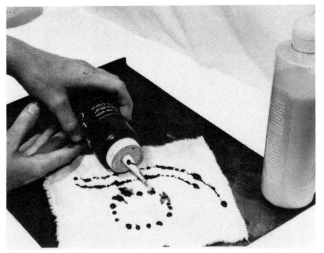

Squeezing Dye *from a plastic bottle directly on the fabric can make either tiny dribbles or heavy lines.*

Museum visits.

T.V. shows and movies.

Graphics. Book covers, wallpaper, posters, and greeting cards.

In general, anything and everything your eye should chance upon can trigger off an inspiration that can be the gateway to a work of art.

Designing

It's hard not to duplicate, at least to some extent, things that have been done in the past, but you can devise new combinations by filtering what you see through your mind's eye.

Certain aspects of design are bound to appeal to you more than others. For example, you may discover that you love Art Nouveau. If so, make the most of it by incorporating lots of Art Nouveau into your work. You'll find that your best work comes from experimenting with the things you love.

Scribbling. Sometimes you may not find any design ideas that interest you. If so, just pick up a pencil and start making scribbles at random. The more you doodle, the more you'll get into it and the better the chances will be for an idea to pop up.

Outlining Objects. Take any ordinary object that's lying around the house—like a plate, a key, or a bottle top. Place it on top of your fabric and draw around its edge. Many exciting designs can be contrived by using single, combined, or overlapping forms.

Making a Viewer. You might want to construct a viewer, or viewfinder, to aid you in spotting a good design. This is a device that is familiar to every art student.

Simply take a small piece of fairly heavy paper or cardboard and cut out a 1″ x 2″ square. Place this over one eye while you're looking at a design or picture. This way you can isolate parts, section by section, to decide which area to use. This method makes it easier to be selective—it doesn't overwhelm you with too much stimuli all at once. You can also achieve the same results by placing your paper or cardboard right on your picture and moving it around until just the right section "hits" you.

Ink Blots. Ink blots, like the type used in Rorschach psychology tests, can be used to advantage. The intricate ink-blot patterns can be translated into design motifs for your batik.

Place a small drop of ink in the middle of a sheet of paper, fold the paper in half or blot with another sheet. A two-sided or irregularly shaped impression will be made. Sometimes the blot will appear formless, while at other times it may suggest a recognizable form.

Folding and Cutting Paper. Another great technique is to use an exercise that's popular among pre-schoolers. Fold a piece of paper two or three times and cut a pattern out of either the corner, the sides, or the center, against or away from the fold. (You can draw the design first with a pencil or start cutting freely, without guidelines.) Use the cut-out paper either as a pattern, by drawing around the outside edges on the cloth, or as a stencil, by drawing along the inside cut. (see Chapter 5).

Objects as Design Ideas

There are many ways to use simple, everyday objects to help pave the way for a creative work. The accompanying photographs show how various objects can be used to their best advantage. Hopefully, these examples will give you an idea of the many possibilities open to exploration.

All the techniques shown involve indelible inks, thickened dyes, or fabric pigments applied to cloth in some way by certain objects. The unique character of

Wire Mesh *placed over paper then dabbed with paint, will give you a motley screenlike effect.*

Drybrush *by whisking a semi-dry brush across a page for an interesting impression.*

Pipe Cleaners *dipped in paint can make imprints on paper, or they can be dipped in dye and used on the fabric.*

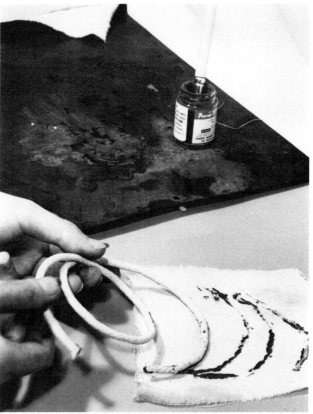

Rope *can also be dipped in ink or paint and flattened on the surface of the paper.*

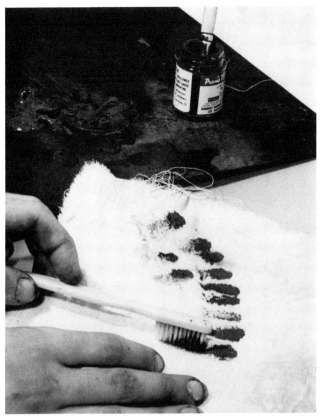

A Toothbrush can be dipped in paint and either pressed to the fabric or held above the fabric so you can strike the bristles with a pencil to create droplets.

Paper Cutouts made from folding and cutting paper create very attractive repeat patterns.

A Tea Strainer filled with dye can make interesting dribbles and dots when moved over the fabric.

Doilies, either plastic or paper, can be used in the same manner as a stencil.

Books *(Above) have unbelievable worlds of design trapped within them. All that's needed is a bit of searching and some imagination.*

Ink Blots *are simply made by dropping ink on paper and folding.*

the particular object used will determine the type of design or line made on the cloth. Any of these techniques can be used if a batik is at its idea stage or in an evolving stage of dyeing, just as long as wax doesn't interfere with the adhesion of the color.

How to Use Batiks

Here is a list of ways to use your batiked fabric for serviceable purposes:

Decorate jeans with colorful batik patches

All types of clothing—formal and informal

Belts

Scarfs

Headbands

Pillows

Quilts and bedspreads

Pocketbooks

Murals and pictures

Lampshades

Stuffed animals and toys

Bookmarks

Three-dimensional hangings

Decorate hinged screens

Greeting cards, writing paper, and envelopes

Mobiles

Curtains

Eggs

Room dividers

Desk sets

Eyeglass cases

Decorate boxes and jewelry cases

Mirror and picture frames

Stuffed batik furniture

Soft sculpture

Whole room environments

India's Dream by Joanifer, 4 x 2¼ feet. Blue, orange, purple, and yellow dyes give this Far Eastern temple fantasy its vibrant effect.

4
TRANSFERRING AND REPRODUCING DESIGNS

In this chapter you'll find out how to transfer your ideas onto cloth. You'll also learn that most of the methods can be used again and again to reproduce your work. Batiks can't be reproduced down to the finest line of crackle, but the main design concept can be followed through.

Tracing Paper

Tracings can be used not just to copy a whole design, but also to trace those intricate details you're hesitant to draw directly on the cloth. This method makes even beginners feel like pros and enables them to work with confidence.

Suppose you want a detailed flower pattern on a dress, and you've found just the design you need in a book. Place your tracing paper over the design and copy it directly. Then you can transfer the design onto the fabric as described later in this chapter.

Thin Fabric

Thin fabric tracings are by far the easiest and most convenient way to both copy and transfer designs.

The technique involves purchasing fabric that's thin enough to see through to the area you're copying. Unbleached muslin or cotton will usually be perfect, but if you want to be sure, take whatever you'll be copying right along to the fabric shop and place the fabric over it. This way you'll know if the fabric will let enough light through to be useful. You can place the fabric directly over a book page if the size of the design doesn't need altering. You can also put it over a sketch or tracing you've done if the lines are dark enough to show through.

Sometimes I've had to reproduce very intricate batiks and found it saves time to place the thinner fabric directly over the batik to be copied. You can quickly make several copies this way. One drawback, however, is that for some batiks you'll naturally want to have thicker cloth. This is especially true if the work is rather large and you plan to hang it freely—without a frame. The solution is to go ahead and use thin fabric and back it with a thicker fabric when it's finished. Chapter 16 will give you more ideas on backing your work.

Carbon Sheets

It's sometimes faster to draw something freehand than to go to all the trouble of tracing paper and carbons. But if your drawing is shaky or you can't spend the necessary time, then you've got to use them.

Arranging the Fabric. To make a carbon transfer, put a piece of fabric on a hard, flat surface, like a linoleum kitchen floor or a smooth table (for large work, a spacious floor area is best). Never use a floor area covered by a rug or you'll get an uneven transfer. Floor boards will make line indentations in your work, so a smooth surface is essential.

Placing the Carbon. Take the carbon and place it *glossy side down* on top of the fabric. This is very important because otherwise no impression will be made.

All portions of the design must be covered with carbon if they are to be transferred. If the drawing's particularly large, you might have to use several sheets. Make sure that no two sheets overlap each other, however, or the design won't show up in those areas. You can also use only one sheet, but you have to keep moving it to correspond to the spot you're working on.

Trace Your Design. Next make a tracing of the design you plan to use, or get out the sketch you've made on regular paper. Place this on top of the carbon in the exact position you want. Tape down both the carbon and tracing sheet(s) with masking tape at all four corners. You might tape the cloth as well so it won't slip.

The Transfer. Bear down firmly on the pencil and go over each line on your paper. Check underneath the carbon now and then to make sure all lines are showing up with equal intensity. If not, slip the carbon back into place and go over the lines again, but don't bear down too hard this time or the paper will rip apart.

Hints. After making your transfers, you may want to save the carbon paper to use again. Tracing paper usually lasts through three copyings before becoming

Carbon Transfer

Step 1. *Draw your design on paper or fabric. Then place the fabric to be batiked on a hard surface and put the carbon paper on top of it.*

bedraggled. Regular bond lasts longer. But if you want to save a complex design to use again, transfer to new paper while all the details are still intact.

You must take care that the carbon, after much usage, still has its strength. If not, get a new sheet. Fresh carbons make the best transfers.

Dressmaker's Carbon Paper

Another way to transfer designs is to get hold of a package of dressmaker's carbon paper and a tracing wheel. These are sold in many department stores and sewing centers.

The main difference between dressmaker's carbon and regular carbon paper is the color. Carbon paper is black or blue, while dressmaker's carbons vary in color and should be used in contrast to the fabric's color. For instance, if you're batiking a light-colored cloth, choose a carbon that contrasts enough to show up, but doesn't appear too dark. Otherwise it might show up on the final product. When using a darker fabric, use a light-colored carbon.

Most carbon lines will be obscured in the final dye bath, but dressmaker's carbons make sure of it, just as long as you've matched up the color tones well.

The main advantage of the tracing wheel is that it covers lines to be copied much faster than a pencil. Just run the wheel over all the long lines in your work; don't bother with the shorter ones, which you can more easily attack with a pencil. Use the wheel only with dressmaker's carbon—it is thicker than regular carbon and won't tear with pressure.

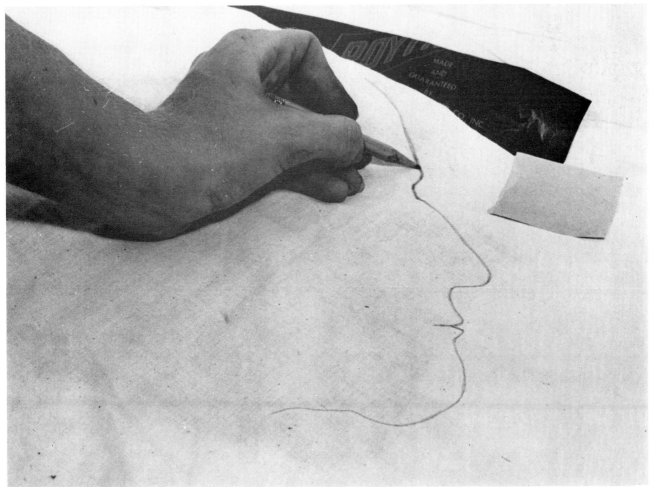

Step 2. *Lay your design on top of the carbon and tape down all three elements securely. Then draw firmly over the design so it will be transferred to the bottom fabric.*

A Pin Stencil. *Draw a design on paper and put an acetate sheet over it. With a large, sharp needle, punch holes through the acetate all along the lines of your design. Then proceed to transfer as described in the text.*

Pin Stencils

These work well for small transfers. Forget about larger transfers with this method unless you're a glutton for punishment—it's too time consuming. Pin stencils also work well if you plan to repeat designs many times (for example, if you want to batik a number of scarfs or hankerchiefs with the same design) because a stencil won't fall apart as fast as carbon paper.

To make a pin stencil, merely place a single sheet of clear acetate (or any other transparent plastic) over your design and tape down the corners of both the design and the acetate. Then take a large rug or upholstery needle and punch holes that correspond to the markings of the design. The holes should be close together, but need not overlap. It's something like playing a "follow the dots" game. Only everything is connected.

The next step is to rub over the outline holes with a bag filled with charcoal. You can purchase one already made or make your own from a piece of cheesecloth or an old stocking. You can also run chalk over the holes, or use a small-pointed brush filled with color.

Be careful not to scatter grains of chalk or charcoal when removing the acetate, or smudging may occur. When you're finished, wash off any charcoal or color that's left on the acetate.

Light Box

This device is also called a "Lacey Luci," and it's good either for tracing or converting sizes. It's basically a machine with a light inside which can be adjusted to enlarge or shrink any design or picture to a given size. Naturally, it's limited to the dimensions set within the confines of the box.

Place thin material (only thin material will work) on top of the box and adjust the size to regulate what you want. The design goes inside the box, and the light inside projects the image from the paper onto the cloth. You could borrow a Lacey Luci from an art school, but since they're heavy to move it's best to ask permission to use it there.

You can also improvise a light box of your own. Of course it won't be able to change sizes like the Lacey Luci, but it will serve its purpose.

Be sure there's a light socket nearby. Take an old pane of glass (you may have one in your basement) and place it between two chairs, or a couple of old boxes. Place a lamp with a 100 watt lightbulb underneath, making sure that the glass is elevated enough so that the light can fit underneath easily. Put the fabric on top of the glass, and sandwich the design between the glass and fabric to make the transfer.

Opaque Projector

This is excellent for large projects like wall murals. There is one big advantage to an opaque projector; it permits you not just to copy a batik cloth design, but to translate any other medium to cloth easily. The one drawback is that you must have a 33mm slide of the design or piece of artwork you want to copy.

Borrow an opaque projector, if you don't already own one, and follow the regular procedure for viewing slides in a darkened room. Either put up a viewing screen, use an empty white wall, or tape a large sheet to a wall. Tape your fabric to your screen, and copy directly from the image being projected.

Avoid making copies of intricate work, as it's often not appreciated on so large a scale. Big, bold designs, however, look smashing.

There is also a machine called an overhead projector that will allow you to insert small pictures from books or magazines instead of slides. These too are often available in schools.

Hip Scene *by Mari Eagerton. This pictorial study of a girl relaxing among swirling floral patterns is a good example of flat decorative designs that could be done with stencils.*

5
STENCILS

A stencil is a time-saving device used for transferring and duplicating designs on cloth or paper. Here are some different types of stencils that are frequently used. You might want to try out each one to see which technique benefits your batiks the most.

Ordinary tracing paper is good to use, for it can be placed over an original drawing or a pattern in a design book for quick reproduction. Stronger papers, however, will hold up better if you're going to be doing any number of batiks with the same motif. Acetate or other transparent sheets also work well for stencils; their transparency makes it easy to copy a design, and they can be used over and over again.

Procedure

Here's what you do in order to make a stencil: first draw your design, then tape it down on top of cardboard or any other surface you don't mind cutting into. Using an X-acto knife, cut out the areas of the design that you want to color.

You may want to use several stencils on one batik, depending on the number of colors it's to have. Keep your knife really sharp when you're cutting out these stencils, so they'll cut easily and have smooth edges.

Attach the completed stencil to your cloth with masking tape. Now you either roll or hand-paint the color on the stencil. You can also paint on a resist if you want any cut-out areas to be protected from the applications of color. A third way to apply color is to draw around the inside lines of the areas you've cut out. Then lift up the stencil and wax the design, following the guidelines closely. Next apply whatever color you want and redye if necessary until the right color combination has been reached.

To add crackle to the batik, wax over the whole cloth and crumple the fabric once the wax is cool. Submerge the fabric in a dye bath and remove the wax in just the same way as when doing a traditional batik.

Contact Paper

Contact paper can also be used to make a stencil. It is available by the roll at most hardware and grocery stores. Buy a plain, solid color, without patterns. Unfortunately, this material is too thick for tracing, so you must draw directly on it in pencil or pen. You can, however, make a light pencil sketch first, as it can be erased if you make a mistake. Next, cut out your design with an X-acto. Peel off the protective paper backing to expose the sticky side, register where you want it to go, and then stick it down slowly on top of the cloth. When you're finished you can pull it off and save it by sticking it on a plastic sheet.

Step 1. *Draw your design on paper and cut out the shapes with an X-acto knife.*

Step 2. *Put the stencil over your fabric and tape it down securely. Then apply either textile paint or dye with a brush.*

Step 3. *Wax over the whole fabric, crumple, and dye in the same manner as a regular batik, then remove the wax.*

Templates

A template is merely the cut-out portion (or inside) of a stencil. You should save these insides—you can draw around the outsides and later wax just the outlines with a tjanting or fill in with color.

After doing your initial design, you can save all your stencils and templates for other batik projects. You should clean any stray paint off the stencils so they'll stay in good condition.

More Pointers

Don't apply very hot wax to stencil edges or it will run underneath them and damage your design. This also goes for paints and dyes—apply them thinly and carefully. If treated with respect, stencils can be used repeatedly.

You may need to make several stencils to cover a large batik. If so, you can either tape them together or attach them singly, but in either case attach them firmly so they won't slide around and confuse matters.

If you're working a very large piece you can buy large rolls of white stencil paper from a paper house. By unrolling it a bit at a time, you can adjust it to fit your bolt of cloth.

Prasad for Everyone,
the finished product,
is simple in design
but quite striking.

Batiks Unlimited. *Here are some of the many decorative and practical ways you can display your batiks.*

6
COLOR
CONSIDERATIONS

An understanding of color is essential when making a batik. In fact, a creative use of color can make or break your work, because color is an all-important part of the batik process. Hopefully you'll find out enough "color basics" in this chapter to start you on the rainbow road of color creativity.

Primary Colors. Red, yellow, and blue. When mixed together they create all other colors. Just be sure that they're absolutely pure when mixing, or you won't get a clear color.

Secondary Colors. Made from equal amounts of any two primaries. For example, yellow and green make blue; blue and red make violet.

Intermediate Colors. Mixtures of primary and secondary colors. For example, red and orange will give you red-orange.

Complementary Colors. Any two colors that when combined yield gray or gray-black. Orange and blue or red and green are good examples.

Color Value

The value of a color is changed when you add black, gray, or white to the original hue. Black and white are neutral and don't change the color as such, only it's lightness and darkness. Contrasts can be sharp or subdued depending on how much of a neutral is added. The purest colors are found in the color-prism because they reflect the most light. The addition of a neutral thus changes the amount of light reflected.

Intensity

Intensity is the purity of light mirrored in a color. Be very careful if you plan to use colors of equal intensity close together. When equally intense colors are near each other, they may appear harsh and overwhelm the eye (red and green, for example). These color combinations can be softened by changing values or neutralizing intensity.

When white or black is added to a color, the intensity decreases. But in the first case the value is lightened, while in the other it is darkened.

Warm and Cool Colors

The warm colors are red, orange, and yellow, and they remind us of the sun; the cool colors, blue, violet, and green, relate to the sky and water. It's good to be especially aware of this when you're trying to "set a mood."

For example, it would be natural to do a hot, summer beach scene with a

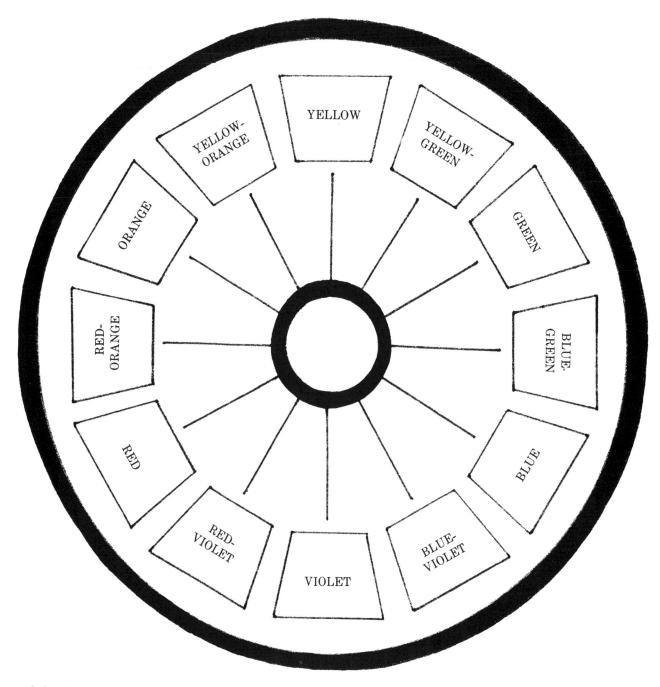

Color Wheel *developed by Faber Birren. This wheel shows at a glance how all the basic hues relate to one another.*

COLOR CHART FOR OVERDYEING

DYE COLOR	OVER RED PRODUCES	OVER BLUE PRODUCES	OVER YELLOW PRODUCES	OVER BROWN PRODUCES	OVER ORANGE PRODUCES	OVER GREEN PRODUCES	OVER PURPLE PRODUCES
Red	Darker Red	Purple	Scarlet	Reddish Brown	Light Red	Dull Brown	Reddish Purple
Blue	Purple	Deep Blue	Green	Very Dark Brown	Dull Dark Gray	Bottle Green	Bluish Purple
Yellow	Scarlet	Green	Deep Yellow	Golden Brown	Yellow Orange	Light Green	Greenish Brown
Brown	Brownish Red	Almost Black	Yellowish Brown	Darker Brown	Yellowish Dark Brown	Greenish Brown	Chocolate
Orange	Red	Dull Dark Gray	Light Orange	Tobacco Brown	Deep Orange	Yellowish Green	Reddish Brown
Green	Almost Black	Greenish Blue	Light Green	Olive Drab	Myrtle Green	Darker Green	Dull Dark Gray
Purple	Reddish Purple	Plum	Almost Black	Very Dark Reddish Brown	Light Dull Purple	Dull Dark Purple	Darker Purple

EXAMPLE: Pink over Light Blue produces Lavender

Pink over Light Yellow produces Shell Pink

Pink over Light Orange produces Coral Pink

The original color (unless white or off-white) will always affect the color you are dyeing. Dark dye shades of Red, Blue, Green, etc. will usually cover light shades of other colors.

To dye fabric Black:
Over Green, Brown, or Yellow, use one package Putnam's Navy Blue for each two or three packages Putnam's Black.

Over Red or Purple, use one package Putnam's Forest Green or Olive Green for each two or three packages Putnam's Black.

Over Blue, use one package Putnam's Orange for each package Putnam's Black.

If too much Black is used, material will have a brownish cast.

PUTNAM DYES, INC.
Quincy, Ill. 62301

The Eye of God by Joanifer. This futuristic crayon batik combines surrealism with balanced design.

A Forest Happening *by Mari Eagerton.*
This work shows a creative use of wax to
achieve minute vegetative detail. An over-
all feeling of fairy-tale communion can be
sensed between the animals.

color scheme of all warm colors. On the other hand, an underwater scene or a sophisticated abstract could look perfect if enhanced with cool colors. Both warm and cool colors can be contrasted for brilliant effects. It's up to the individual craftsman to decide which combinations work best for him.

Composition

When planning a color composition, try to think in terms of a totality instead of single areas. This will provide your design with a "unity," where everything will fit together naturally.

No one color should be prized for its merit alone, but only in view of its relationship to other colors. If a composition is well-organized, balanced, and has a variety of line and color, it can't fail to be appealing.

Planning a Batik

Pre-planning the colors you'll use is one of the most important aspects of making a batik. You'll either want to use dyes in their original shade, or mix different ones together for a variety of hues. If you're dyeing cloth in the "traditional" way, it's wise to make a preliminary sketch first on paper. This can be colored with crayons or pencils, or just labeled with the names of each color. Each time a new color is dyed, you can fill in or cross out these areas. This way confusion about which colors have been dyed is eliminated.

You can dispense with this preparation when you use fabric paints or dyes for painting directly on the cloth. There's no confusion about what hue goes where, unless you decide to combine the painting with traditional waxing and dye submersion.

The Color Wheel

The color wheel shown on page 60 shows a system of color standardization developed by Faber Birren. The system is composed of 13 hues, and each is based on Birren's belief that all colors are merely mixtures of three qualities: hue, black, and white.

Note carefully how the colors are arranged. Each forms a relationship to the other according to their position on the wheel. It can easily be seen that yellow, red, and blue (the primaries) form an upright triangle, while orange, green, and violet (the secondaries) form an upside-down triangle. The intermediate colors are in between. Colors directly opposite each other are complementary. Split-complements can be found by taking a key color, such as orange, and finding its opposite. The colors (blue-green and blue-violet in this case) on either side of this opposite are both complementary to it. The warm colors are grouped together at the top and to the left of the color wheel, while the cool are at the bottom and to the right.

Putnam Color Chart

The color chart shown on page 61 will help you make the most of dyeing one color on top of another, or "overdyeing" as it's called.

The colors listed will vary slightly from manufacturer to manufacturer, but the basic shades are similar enough to make this chart handy for general color information.

There's no way to predict exactly to the letter how one color will look on top of another, however, because each successive color influences the ones beneath it. Still, if you have at least a rough idea of what to expect, you're ahead of the game. Also, don't forget to take a good look at the color wheel.

Last Embrace by Joanifer, 60" x 36". Here batik has been integrated into an oil painting to produce an unusual and effective collage. The painting was done first, then cotton cloth was batiked, cut into shapes, and glued to the canvas to accent areas of the royal garments.

5

6

7

1. The Bird's Message, *30" x 36". A romantic modern version of the Garden of Eden. Batiked unbleached muslin was stretched on a frame, bordered with wood strips, and stained with walnut varnish.*

2. Priests, *28" x 40". This traditional batik also suggests the three Magi. Portions of the robes were wet down before the dye was applied by hand, resulting in a muted, misty look much like that found in Japanese watercolors.*

3. The Unicorn Knows, *28" x 38". This shows traditionally batiked cloth accented with hand-painted details. It was framed on a stretcher to convey the "total" look of a period painting.*

4. The Council of the King, *38" x 43". Another romantic batik with a fairytale quality. The effects were achieved by many dippings in various-colored dye baths.*

5. Rama's Journey, *80" x 65". This relatively large work reflects the folklore and legends of ancient India.*

6. Forest Ballad, *48" x 36". A batik such as this could easily illustrate an Old English fable; it conveys the feeling of, "In days of old when knights were bold..."*

7. Lovers' Embrace, *26" x 35". A batik with a medieval flavor. Stencils were used for the outlines of the trees and suns, and dyes were dripped directly onto some areas to produce decorative dots.*

The batiks on these two pages are all by Joanifer.

Egyptian Musicians *by Joanifer, 50″ x 42″. This is an example of a hand-painted batik. Thick textile paints were applied directly with a brush, and the outlines were drawn with indelible ink.*

Dragon Meets the Lady *by Joanifer, 48″ x 37½″. This multicolored batik went through several overdyeings before it was finished. After de-waxing, the intricate details of the figure and dragon scales were added with a fine-pointed brush.*

Kitchen Wall Hanging by Lillian Donald, 78″ x 108″. This tie-dye is carefully styled in eye-pleasing colors. Note the areas where the cloth was folded in segments and tied off separately, producing a special quality of symmetry.

M.A. #4 by Lillian Donald, 146″ x 37″. This tie-dye is primarily composed of circular forms, which shows that the fabric was gathered and tied off countless times before dyeing.

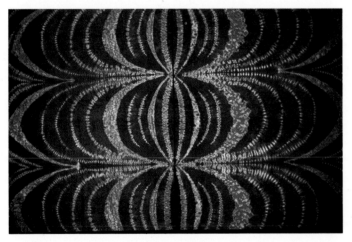

M.A. #5 by Lillian Donald, 102″ x 222″. This photo shows only one portion of this tie-dye's vast yardage. It is reminiscent of solar system energy branching out in waves of cosmic conciousness.

Red-Blue Sunrise by Lillian Donald, 34″ x 70″. This photo shows a detail of a silk hanging, gloriously decorated by tie-dyeing. The combination of method and material produces fascinating patterns in both stable formation and in radiating, fanlike attitudes.

Ukranian Eggs by Sophia Mychajlyshyn (left). These exquisite eggs were all created in the traditional Ukranian fashion. This age-old art uses the batik method of wax resist for applying color.

Sufi Dervish *by Joanifer, 25" x 36". A "double-method" batik: melted crayons were brushed on for the intricate skirt design, while traditional dyeing methods give other parts their color.*

7
CRAYON BATIK

Now let's examine crayon batik, or encaustic painting as it's sometimes called. This will be our first digression from the "traditional process." To make a crayon batik, you'll be using ordinary crayons (the same kind used for children's coloring books) right along with batik dye and wax.

Actually crayons are nothing more than colored wax, but when melted along with batik wax (or paraffin) and applied to fabric, they become magical. The crayon-wax combination colors the cloth as it seeps into the fibers. When the wax hardens, the fabric is crumpled, then dumped into a dye bath. This bath lets liquid dye go into the cracked areas (as well as dyeing the background areas), to give that added veined effect that makes batiks sparkle.

Crayon batik is really a two-in-one process. The principle once again is wax resist, just as it was for traditional batik, but the wax crayon itself acts as a coloring agent.

Advantages

Crayon batik has definite advantages over the traditional process. I don't want to play favorites, however, for each process is unique, and satisfying.

Color Selection. The color selection available in crayons today is astounding. Pick up any well-known brand (Crayola or Rembrandt for example) and you won't believe your eyes.

Time. With crayon batik you won't have to wait for the cloth to dry between dye baths because there's only one dye bath at the end of the process. You'll be able to completely finish a piece in one sitting, and it will look as if you went through all of the "traditional" processes.

Cost. You won't need to buy many dyes for crayon batik. You'll only be using one dye bath, and in the long run, crayons cost less than dyes. Also, the hardened wax mixture can be reheated and used again and again, just as can any wax used for traditional batiking.

Two Batiks in One. Before you iron out the wax from your batik, place a sheet of paper (any type will do) underneath your fabric. As you iron, the heat will transfer the colored wax image to the paper below. This design will be soft and muted, with a special Oriental delicacy that you may find just as appealing as your original fabric.

Limitations

This new process has its drawbacks, so consider them carefully before you begin work. First of all, when crayon colors are applied to cloth, the colors are often not as vivid as dye colors. Later on in this chapter I'll tell you how to overcome this problem. Color-fastness can also be a problem, so always dry-clean with this process. Another problem is that, as with traditional batik, wax sometimes falls away when the fabric is crumpled in the dye bath. This causes dye to seep into the exposed areas, obscuring your design. You'll find out how to solve this later.

Equipment

Here's a list of the materials you'll need. You've used some of them before in traditional batik, and you'll meet them again in the pages that follow.

Crayons. To start out, you'll need a box of basic spectrum colors. These colors can be mixed together to make other shades. As you progress, you'll probably want to try out some of the more bizarre shades. Luckily, most art stores as well as five and dimes carry a huge selection of colors.

Crayon sizes vary, too. You can buy large ones either separately or boxed together in groups of one or several different colors. I suggest buying a few extra-large crayons for those big expanses like sky, land, and background areas.

Batik Wax or Paraffin. Either one can be added to the crayons. As you recall from Chapter 1, batik wax contains more paraffin than beeswax, but still won't produce as many cracks as pure paraffin. Therefore, if you want a lot of crackle, then use the paraffin; for fewer cracks, and less color, use the batik wax.

Melting Containers. Cupcake containers make great melting pots for crayons. It's nice to have two sizes, but that's not a must (if you're using an electric skillet, however, only a small container will fit inside). Both small and large pans have 12 individual cups. If you like, you can break up the smaller crayons in the small cups and the larger ones in the bigger holders. It's best to keep the sizes separated, so you can measure out equal proportions of wax to crayons.

Two medium-sized saucepans are handy also. One is for melting batik wax and the other for paraffin, should you decide to use them.

Skillet, Oven, or Hot Plate. A skillet works like a double-boiler, only you can control the temperature (it should be between 120° and 140°). Only small cupcake tins will fit inside the skillet.

The same holds true for a hot plate; its surface just isn't large enough for a big tin to fit comfortably. So for large cupcake pans, use the oven, but make sure it's set at its lowest temperature.

Both the hot plate and the oven heat up wax super-fast, so keep a close watch to see that the wax doesn't get *too* hot *too* fast. Ideally, the skillet with controlled heating is the best device to use.

Miscellaneous. The rest of the equipment for crayon batik—fabric, brushes, dyes, etc.—are just the same as those used in the traditional process. Refer back to Chapter 1 for more information.

Procedure

Now I'll explain the various steps involved in the crayon batik process. The demonstration nearby will give you a visual explanation as well. The first step is to prepare your fabric by washing or boiling (or both). Then transfer your design or draw it right on the fabric (see Chapter 1 for more details).

Preparing the Crayons. Unwrap your crayon sticks, one at a time. Then break the crayons up into small pieces and toss them into the cups. You can put two or more crayons into each cup, but it shouldn't be over half full because an equal amount of batik wax (or paraffin) has to fit in, too. Also, when these substances melt, the level of liquid will rise.

As you prepare each color, it's a good idea to write its name on a piece of masking tape with a felt-tip marker. Stick the tape underneath the cup containing that color so you'll know which color is which.

The Crayon Batik Process

Step 1. *Prepare the fabric by washing it in soap and water.*

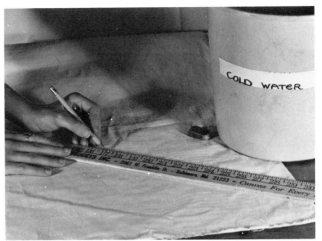

Step 2. *Transfer the design or draw it directly on the fabric.*

Step 3. *Unwrap the desired crayons and break them into small pieces. Put the pieces, color by color, into labeled cupcake tins.*

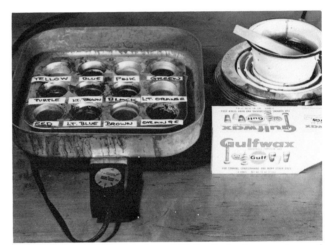

Step 4. *Melt the crayons in a skillet set at a temperature of 300° F. Heat batik wax at the same time in a saucepan. Both should be melted 6 to 8 minutes.*

Step 5. *Slowly pour the batik wax into the liquid crayons and stir well. There should be equal amounts of each.*

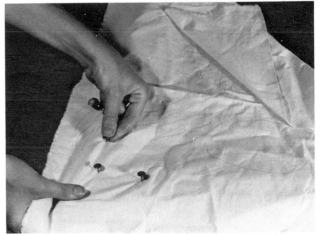

Step 6. *Position the fabric by tacking it to a stretcher.*

Step 7. *Paint on the liquid crayons with a brush, making sure the wax penetrates through to the back of the fabric.*

Step 8. *Crumple the cloth and submerge it in water to cool and harden the wax.*

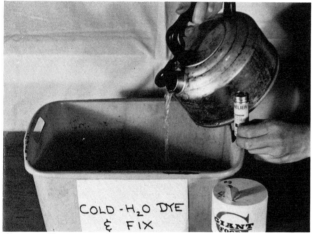

Step 9. *Prepare a dye solution in the traditional manner.*

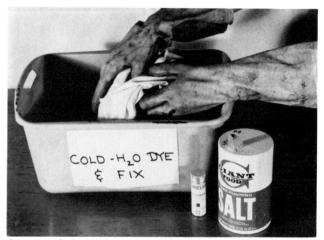

Step 10. *Submerge the fabric in the dye bath until the desired color is reached.*

Step 11. *Remove the wax by the iron-cut method.*

Fish Fantasy, *the completed batik.*

Melting the Wax. Melt a one-pound package of paraffin or batik wax in a pan at the same time as you melt the crayons. This speeds up the process and saves a great deal of time.

Place the cupcake tin inside an electric skillet containing 2″ or 3″ of water and set the thermostat to between 120° and 140°F. As the water heats, the crayons will melt. You can also begin heating the water ahead of time so the crayons will melt faster.

Another way to prepare wax is to chip or break off pieces and melt these right along with the crayons.

Your wax and crayons should be completely melted in 6 or 8 minutes (or less, depending on which device you're using). You can tell they're both ready when smoke starts to drift slowly off the top, or when your candy thermometer hits between 120° to 140°F.

Combining Wax and Crayons. Carefully pour the melted batik wax (or paraffin) into the liquid crayons in the cupcake tin. Since you need equal amounts of each, it will probably be easiest to use a spoon, unless you've got an especially steady hand for pouring just the right amount. Average about 3 or 4 teaspoons of wax per regular-size crayon and slightly more wax for larger crayons. Mix both ingredients well, either with your spoon or wooden stick.

Position the Fabric. Now you're ready to apply the hot wax solution to the fabric. First decide if you'll be using wax paper underneath the cloth to catch the wax, or if you want to tack it to canvas stretchers. You can also clamp one end of it inside a washing machine, as was discussed in Chapter 1.

Applying the Wax. The important thing to remember about applying wax is that it *must* penetrate all the way through to the back of the cloth. I can't stress this enough, especially in regard to crayon batik. The color of crayons can be deceptive—it often looks as if it has been absorbed by the cloth, when in reality it has merely touched the surface. Keep checking the back of the fabric to make sure that the color has soaked through evenly.

Have your cupcake tin of colored wax really close to the fabric for quick application. Don't hesitate between dipping your brush in the pan and applying the wax to the fabric. If you dally an extra second, the melted crayon colors won't be hot enough to go through to the back of the cloth.

Be very careful with small details. Touch the brush tip gently to the fabric, because the hotter the wax gets, the faster it spreads on contact. Although streaming-hot wax is essential, you shouldn't overcharge your brush for detailed work, or fast-moving wax will run rampant over those delicate lines. For bigger areas this won't be a problem, so you can load up your brush with as much wax as you want and apply it with vigor.

Before dipping your brush into each new cup of melted crayons, wipe the excess color off the bristles with a paper towel. Do this while the wax is still hot, so the remaining wax will glide off easily. If the color on the brush has been allowed to cool and becomes too hard to remove, simply stick the brush back into the same hot wax solution; the wax will become soft and you can rub it off gently with a paper towel. This procedure will eliminate the problem of muddy colors. Hardly a trace of color will remain on the brush and certainly not enough to foul the other color mixtures.

Another tip about applying wax: if you want a true, deep tone, be sure to stir each color well before applying. The crayon's pigment sinks to the bottom almost immediately upon melting. If you *want* a weaker color, however, don't stir, but dip the brush gingerly just into the top of the colored wax in the tin. This will give you a pastel effect.

It's important to note that any areas to remain white (or the original color of the fabric) should first be painted with clear batik wax or paraffin. This will protect the white surface from the final dye bath. For a bright, vivid white you can use a melted white crayon.

If the dye color you choose for the crackle—or the color of the last dye bath—also happens to appear as a color anyplace else in the design, then leave this area exposed. When the fabric is immersed in the dye bath it will receive its color right along with the cracks.

Dyeing the Fabric. Cool the wax normally at room temperature (or place the cloth in the refrigerator if you want wax to harden quickly). Crunch the fabric up well with your hands if you want a lot of crackle. For just a few cracks, simply dip the fabric in the dye solution with as little folding as possible. (For more information on dyeing refer back to Chapter 1.)

Wax Removal. Use either an electric iron, a cleaning solvent, boiling, or dry-cleaning to get out that ground-in wax. Turn back once more to Chapter 1 for full details and the pros and cons of each technique.

Problems and Solutions

Here are some of the problems (along with their solutions) that you might encounter with this technique:

Overflowing Pans. Even though crayons will eventually be melted down into liquid, you've still got to break them up into pieces so they'll fit into the cupcake tins. If you throw them whole into the tins haphazardly, they will stick out and melt all over the sides, making a big mess for you to clean up. The best idea is to put small crayons into small tins and large crayons into big ones. Be consistent. Never break up small crayons in the first few cups and then forget and put larger ones in other cups. When melting begins, the small crayons will be fine, but the larger ones may spill out all over creation.

When you need lots of one color, either use the larger tins or an old saucepan. If you know you'll be doing several large batiks with the same colors, then these pans are essential. Buy several boxes of crayons of the same hue and break the entire boxful into a pan. Do the same for each new color. This way there will be more than enough to finish the whole job.

This is also a good idea if you plan to use a fair amount of an unusual color. Otherwise, halfway through the project, you might run out of a color that may be hard to duplicate.

Breaking Up Wax. You can break up the batik wax (or paraffin) into chunks before melting, but you must be able to judge how many chips are needed to balance with the amount of crayons you're using. Chapter 1 fully explains how to chip off wax into even pieces with a hammer and screwdriver.

If you find it hard to break the wax up into uniform chunks, then it's easier to melt the wax separately in a saucepan before pouring it in with the crayons.

Regulating Temperature. Temperature regulation can be a problem if you use a hot plate; there's no temperature gauge to turn down if the wax gets too hot. The only thing to do is to lift the cupcake tin off the heat if the smoke vapors start to rise too quickly. You may have to do this quite often because the hotter the wax, the more it smokes. Don't forget to put on mitts or use a pot holder!

Another problem with the hot plate is that heat is concentrated in the center. This means that the cups in the middle will heat fastest, while the wax in the outside cups may still be fairly solid. You'll have to keep moving the tin slightly so all cups get their share of warmth.

Both the skillet and the oven have temperature controls that can be adjusted. If you're using an oven, do keep checking inside to see when the wax is ready. You'll have to take the wax out when it gets too hot and return it when it cools. This will really keep you on your toes, because it cools almost as fast as it heats up.

Wax Fumes. As I've mentioned before, always wax in a well-ventilated area; it's not healthy to breath in too many waxy fumes.

Wax Flaking. If too much wax flakes off during the dye bath, these unprotected areas will turn the color of the dye. If this happens, get some bleach or a cleaning solvent and dab the dyed area lightly. Repeat the process a second time if the dye is stubborn. You can repaint crayon color over any places that are now bare.

Too Many Cracks. The best way to handle this problem is to prevent it from happening in the first place—use batik wax instead of paraffin and don't crumple the fabric. You may occasionally still run into a few cracks in some areas of your design. If this happens, use a cleaning solvent or bleach after the wax has been removed. You can retouch areas later with colored wax if they seem to need it.

Too Few Cracks. If you want more colored cracks to brighten up your design, wait until the fabric is dry and repaint the whole surface with clear batik wax (or paraffin). Crunch up the fabric and redye in the dye bath. Or you can just rewax and paint the dye into the cracks with brush to save time.

No Cracks. If you don't want any cracks at all, then don't use a final dye bath. There's no point to it unless you have large background areas to fill with color.

Colors Running Together. If too much paraffin or too much batik wax has been added to the crayon mixture in the beginning, the waxed colors will run together, fade out, or spread when the iron hits them. If this happens, iron out all the remaining wax and repaint colored wax over the areas once again. After this very little blurring will occur, for the iron's heat should melt the excess color right out when you've finished.

Note. Try this interesting experiment: rub some crayons over a kitchen grater until they're broken into tiny bits. Scatter them across the cloth and cover with a sheet of paper or another piece of fabric. Then iron over top. Afterwards, you can dump the whole thing into a dye bath. Some very interesting abstract patterns will result.

Lancelot and Guinevere
by Joanifer, 7 x 3¾ feet,
Here legend is colorfully
depicted in batik.

Greek Orthodox *by Joanifer, 2¾ x 2 feet. This scenic batik was dipped in six different dye baths to achieve muted colors and tones. A compass was used to shape the outer halo and cardboard shapes used as models for the trees and rays.*

8

HAND-PAINTED BATIK

This method is by far the quickest and most direct way of creating a batik, and once again you'll get the same beautiful results—as if you'd spent hours dipping the cloth in many separate dye baths.

Don't misunderstand, you can still use the dye bath in combination with direct painting if you want. Or you can dive into this process full steam, and hand-paint the whole batik as you would a canvas painting, then wax and dye.

As with crayon batik, only one final dye bath is needed after the waxing. This will give you the veinlike "crackle" as well as dye any additional portions of your batik the same color as the crackle.

The advantages of this technique are obvious. You don't have to use guesswork about the surprises that overdyeing may have in store for you. Unless you're combining methods, you will know immediately what colors will accept other colors and which will retain their purity.

The Principle

The principle of hand-painted batik is basic and simple. Whenever dyes are applied to cloth by hand and then set by heating, the colors "take" or adhere permanently to the fabric's fibers. Wax is then applied to the whole work and acts as a resist for the last step, which is the dye bath.

Dyes

Special dyes must be used for direct painting on fabric. You just can't paint on any old dye solution that happens to be handy and expect it to be color-fast. The long immersion in a dye bath plus the addition of a mordant helps assure permanent color in traditional dyeing. Direct painting can't rely on these factors, so other materials must be found.

The best dyes to use are called *fiber reactives*. In England, these are available under the trade name Procion. In America, they are available under the trade names Putnam, Fibrec, and Dylon (among others). The dyes are completely color-fast when thickeners are added. Thickeners cause the dye to adhere to the cloth even after many washings, just as long as the dye is set by heat. They can usually be purchased right along with the dyes at art stores.

Always mix your dyes and thickeners according to package instructions before applying them to the prewashed cloth. You can dilute the dye mixture with a few drops of water for easy application.

Fabric Paints

These textile pigments already contain thickeners that adhere the color to the cloth. Two well known brands are Prang (jars) and Deco-Write (tubes). These

Hand Painting Batik

Step 1. *Draw your design on fabric.*

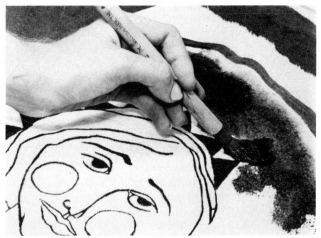
Step 2. *Paint all the areas you want colored with a brush and textile paints.*

Step 3. *Cover the colored areas of the cloth with wax.*

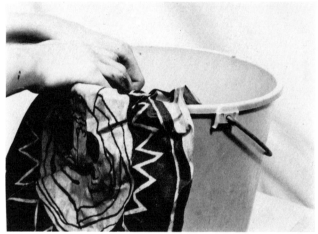
Step 4. *Submerge the fabric in a light-colored dye bath.*

Step 5. *To add crackle, wax the fabric again, crumple it, and spread it on a newspaper-covered floor.*

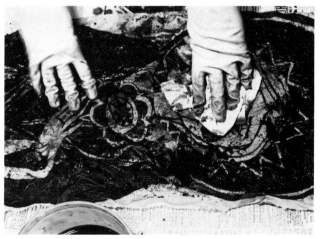
Step 6. *Pour liquid dye on the fabric and work it into the wax cracks. Blot up the excess dye with a rag.*

One Flower for Lisa,
the completed batik,
shows the result of the
hand painting process.

dyes must be heat-fixed by any of the methods described later on in this chapter. Prang offers a wonderful color selection, and they also supply extenders and thinners, both of which thin out paint for easy application. The major difference is that the extenders give more body to your paint. Never add too much of either chemical, however, or the fabric will become stiff.

There are two basic types of textile colors—the transparencies and the opaques. While most colors are transparent, they can be made opaque with the addition of white, because white itself is opaque.

Transparent colors can be compared to glass—they are affected by the underlying color of the cloth. They tend to be brighter and glow more than opaques because of their reflective quality. Opaques are more like china in that they don't reflect light.

When making a traditional batik it is advisable to use only light or fairly pale material. But when hand-painting a batik (unless you're going to be over-dyeing) it doesn't matter. For a darker material you can just add some white to your colors and they'll show up perfectly well. (Again, as with the extender and thinner, don't use too much white or its added thickness will stiffen the cloth.) This doesn't mean that you should go out and randomly buy dark navy or black fabrics, for they'll be a little *too* dark and you will have problems. Use a moderately dark color, for instance a light violet or a medium blue.

Let's face it, the lighter the color of the fabric, the easier it will be to paint on because the colors won't be obscured by the underlying shade.

Other Coloring Agents

There are numerous other coloring agents on the market today besides dyes and textile paints. All of these can be applied to cloth by hand, just as they'd be applied to ordinary paper. You might want to try out each of these singly (or in combination) to see how each can best benefit you: acrylics, indelible inks, felt-tip markers, printing inks, and silkscreen paints are all possibilities. Explore the shelves of your local arts and crafts store and I'm sure you'll find other mediums to experiment with.

Types of Cloth

The best types of cloth to use for direct hand-painting are unbleached muslin, viscose rayon, linen, silk, and mercerized cotton. You can also use any of the other fabrics listed in Chapter 1, but be sure to avoid synthetics.

Fixing or "Setting" Colors

Some dyes, like Fibrec, don't need heat-fixing, but other types of dyes do. The same holds true for pigments. Once again, always check the instructions to be completely sure.

One way to fix your fabric is to lightly iron it on both sides for approximately 5 minutes. If you want you can soak some paper towels in vinegar, wring out the excess, and place the batik between them to iron. This will further help set the colors.

Another method is to use an oven. Roll up the cloth as you would a poster, sandwiched with old newspapers or white paper. This paper should cover the cloth completely so the dye won't rub up against itself. Set the oven at 300° F. and leave the batik in for roughly 5 minutes.

Procedure

This method is a snap and is actually no different from painting a picture on paper with water colors (except that the colors are dyes and fabric paints). The first thing to do, of course, is to draw your design on the fabric.

Painting. There are several ways to apply color to cloth. You can use a brush, or because the dyes and paints will have thickeners added, it may be easier and faster to roll them on with a paint roller or an ink brayer. Rolling will also assure that the color is evenly distributed to all areas of the design.

Both dyes and textile pigments can also be dripped, sprayed, or splattered on cloth. You can spray by loading a brush with color and flicking it with your finger, thus releasing the color onto the cloth. You can drip it from an eye-dropper or squirt it out of a plastic bottle that has a spray attachment.

Waxing. When the fabric colors have completely dried, wax over the entire surface with any type of wax you want (for maximum cracking use paraffin). The wax will act (as it always does) as a resist, not just to one or more areas exclusively, but for the whole piece.

Dyeing the Fabric. When the wax hardens, crush the waxed fabric up well and dump it in a dye bath, in the same way as with the other procedures we've discussed throughout the book.

There is another way to produce "crackle" instead of immersing the cloth in a dye bath, and a bonus is that it takes less time. First spread newspapers on a smooth kitchen or basement floor. (If dye does seep through the paper, mop it up quickly so it won't stain.) Roll, mash, or crunch your waxed material into a tight ball with your hands. This will break up the wax, so cracks will form to let the dye in. Spread the fabric on the floor. When it's lying flat, work the wrinkles out with your hands as much as possible.

Next put on your rubber gloves, and select the dye color for the crackle you want. Slowly pour the liquid dye onto portions of the cloth. Then rub it in well, making sure you've covered all areas. You can wipe off excess dye with a paper towel or tissue in places that you want to stay light—a face or hands for example. When you've finished working the dye into the fibers, return the excess for future use if the brand is re-usable. To salvage the dye, pick up the fabric on either side and bring both sides together to form a funnel. This will let you return the dye to its receptacle with a minimum of spillage.

For a dark crackle, keep rubbing the dye into the waxed cloth for about 5 minutes. For paler shades, you can blot the fabric with towels. Terrycloth towels are especially good because they are extra absorbent.

Waxing Outlines

Another variation of hand-painted batik is to first wax all the outlines of your design. This is a particularly good technique for faces or intricate flower patterns. To make the wax outlines, you can either use a pointed-tip brush or a tjanting. This will protect the underlying surface, which (if white) will result in white outlines. Then you can paint the areas inside the waxed lines by hand with your fabric colors. The final step is to wax and dye the total batik area.

Painting and Dyeing

You may choose to only paint details by brush and dye only those background or very large areas. A rich, beautiful stained-glass effect can be obtained by painting outlines with black dye, fabric paint, India ink, or black felt-tip markers.

After this you can proceed to wax and overdye, just as you did for the traditional process. Background colors or large areas can be dyed right along with the crackle.

Stars Over Norway *by Ralph Friendlich. A bold design makes an attractive batiked, quilted hanging. Gold silk fringe sewn to three edges adds a decorative touch.*

9
RELIEF
PRINTING
BATIK

This process is actually just what it says it is: relief printing combined with batik. It's another innovative, contemporary way to quickly create batiks.

The basic technique is simple. A print is made on the fabric, either before or after it is waxed. The only difference is the preference of the craftsman—the results are the same. As with hand-painted batik, this method can easily be combined with several dye baths.

Printing Before Waxing

I use this method because I've found that the ink sticks more easily to a wax-free surface. First you print your design (the printing process will be explained later in the chapter). Then you cover the whole printed area (or the total surface to be batiked) with wax. Any of the waxes mentioned in Chapter 1 will do, just remember to use lots of paraffin if you want crackle. You can now dye the cloth any shade desired by submersion in a bath, direct pouring, or painting as described in Chapter 6.

Waxing Before Printing

You may have already dyed your cloth once or several times. After this, you'll wax the entire surface of the cloth and dye again for the crackle. Now remove all the wax by ironing, or any of the methods described in Chapter 2.

When you print, it's very important that all the wax be removed or the ink may have trouble sticking to the fabric's surface.

This technique is especially good to use if you're in any way dissatisfied with your original batik. What you may have once considered a real failure can be instantly transformed by just the right overprint design.

Printing Surfaces

There are several well-known substances that everyone has probably printed with at one time or another. It's helpful to know about all of them, as you might want to use one or all in your batik work.

Potato and Eraser Printing

A potato is most commonly used because it's round, easy to handle, and soft for quick carving. But you can also use carrots, apples, or any root vegetable that has a stable body. Onions can be used too, as long as they're washed and you don't mind a few tears. The onion rings will give interesting texture to your work.

To print with a potato, slice it in half, and carve out a simple design with a pen knife. (After carving, only the raised portion that's left behind will print.)

Potato Carving

Step 1. *Carve a design in the potato with an X-acto knife. Remember that only the raised surface will print.*

Step 2. *Ink the potato by dipping a brush in dye, then painting it over the raised design. Use the potato design as a repeated motif on the fabric.*

Because the printing surface is so small, you can ink it by stamping it down on a rubber-stamp pad or simply brush on inks or paints.

Art gum erasers can be printed just like the potato. You follow the exact same printing procedure. When you've finished, you can't tell what type of thing was printed—whether it was an eraser, fruit, or vegetable.

One drawback about printing small surfaces is the amount of time it takes to cover any amount of fabric area. You've got to repeat your pattern or design consecutively over the whole fabric.

Linoleum and Wood Blocks

The main advantage of linoleum and wood is that much larger areas can be covered quickly. You can adjust the size of your printing area to the size of the lino or wood block you're using. You can buy linoleum already mounted on a wooden block at art supply stores, or unmounted at a linoleum or flooring company. For larger works, I find the unmounted kind easier to carve and also to print, because it's not as bulky to handle. You might want to leave your linoleum on top of a radiator for an hour or so before carving, as a little heat will soften it and facilitate carving. You can also put it in the oven at the lowest temperature for about 15 minutes.

Wood can be purchased at a lumberyard, where they'll cut it to size. White pine is the best for carving, because it's tough enough to last through successive printings, but it won't break your fingers off when you dig into it, as some harder wood does.

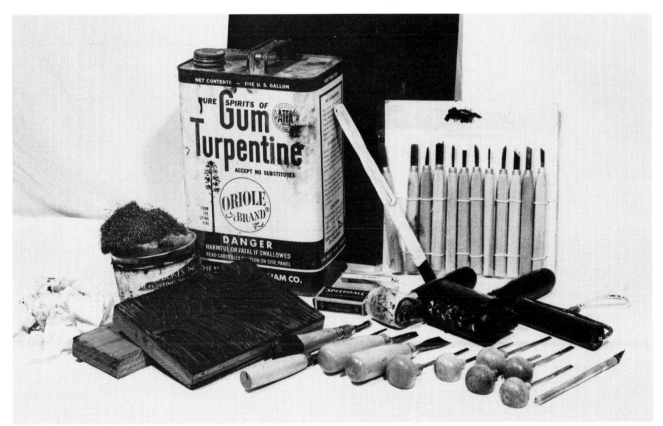

Block Printing Equipment. *The tools you'll need to print include linoleum and wood blocks, knives and gouges, turpentine, printing ink, and rollers or brayers.*

Block Printing

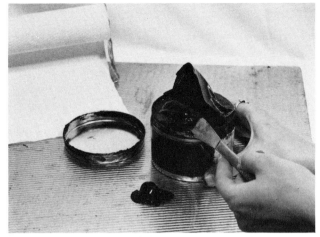

Step 1. Transfer some ink from the can to a cookie sheet and spread it out slightly.

Step 2. Coat your brayer with ink by rolling it back and forth on the inked cookie sheet.

Step 3. Ink your carved block thoroughly, making sure all surfaces are covered.

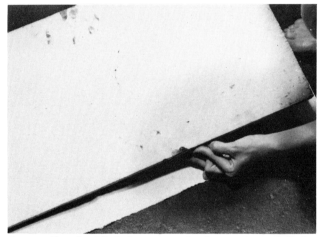

Step 4. Put the fabric face up on the floor and carefully lay the inked block on top of it.

Step 5. Turn the block over (the fabric should stick to the block so they will turn simultaneously).

Step 6. Using a wallpaper roller, roll firmly over the cloth so the ink saturates to the back.

Step 7. *Lift a corner of the cloth to make sure the ink is adhering.*

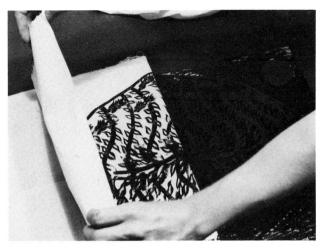

Step 8. *When the print is strong and even, pull the cloth off the block slowly.*

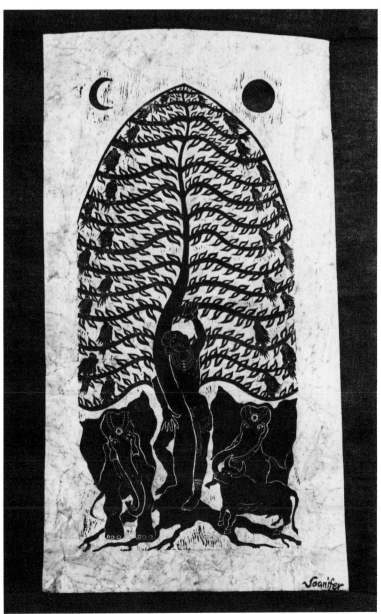

In the Garden of Allah.
This batik-print was waxed, crumpled, and dyed to add some background texture.

Batiked Skirt *made by the block printing process, designed and stitched by the author.*

Batiked Garments *both by Joanifer, show how relief-printed batik can enhance simple styles.*

Equipment

Here is a list of the items you'll find useful to have when you're beginning to print your batik.

Fabric. Avoid printing on heavy fabrics, expecially if they have a nap, because the ink won't sink properly into the fibers, and you'll get that washed out look.

Linoleum or Wood. Both surfaces are ideal for carving—just pick your preference, or try both.

Carving Tools. Different types of chisels and gouges are available for both linoleum and wood. Keep them sharp, so they'll do a good job.

X-acto Knife. This tool is used for wood carving to score lines, making them loose enough to gouge out. Number 11 is the most versatile blade to own.

Printing Inks. Always get the waterproof, oil-based types. These come in many different colors, and are used for linoleum as well as wood printing.

Rubber Brayer. Available in art stores in various sizes, this tool is used for rolling ink onto the printing surface.

Wallpaper Roller. A roller, or an old metal spoon, should be used for rubbing the fabric when it's on top of the printing block to make it accept the ink.

Cookie Sheet. You need a flat, smooth surface to roll the ink out on, and a cookie sheet is ideal for this.

Knife or Spatula. These are handy for scooping ink out of the can, or to spread the ink after squirting it from the tube.

Turpentine, Rags, and Newspapers. For all the cleaning up that's got to be done.

Steel Wool. This is useful for raising the grain on a piece of wood.

Drawing the Design

When you design for block printing, you've got to revamp your thinking, much as you did with batik. Those areas that you don't want to print are carved out, so you'll need to be concerned with balancing the positive and negative spaces. With this in mind, do your drawing (using a 2B pencil). Remember that what you draw will be printed in reverse. To understand this concept hold your completed drawing up to a mirror. This will show you what it will look like after printing. Refer back to Chapter 4 for notes on transferring designs if you want to draw freehand on your blocks.

Carving

Linoleum, being of a soft consistency, carves much faster than wood. That's why beginners usually prefer it. But as you become familiar with wood carving, you may find you like it just as well, or even better than linoleum. Wood has the added advantage of a textured grain, which sometimes shows up in the printing and can create very exciting visual effects.

If your wood has a strongly defined grain, then you may wish to bring the grain out more so it will print clearly. To do this, get some steel wool and turpentine. Slosh the turpentine freely over the grain and rub it down hard with the steel wool. Keep rubbing and dousing with turpentine until the grain starts to rise slightly above the surface. This takes lots of elbow grease, but the printed result is well worth the effort.

When you first start carving you should take your time. The implements are sharp (especially the X-acto knife used for woodcutting) and if they're not used with care you can really hurt yourself.

Printing

The step-by-step procedure for printing on fabric is demonstrated in the photographs nearby.

The first thing to do is to prepare the ink. You can either scoop from a can with a spoon, spatula, or knife, or squeeze out of a tube. Spread the ink around on the cookie sheet, and then coat the brayer. Do this by rolling the brayer firmly into the ink again and again until it's well coated. Run the brayer over the surface of the block until it becomes shiny and almost sparkles with bits of ink. It lets you know if it's ready by starting to feel sticky. Put your fabric face-up on the floor, or any other hard surface. The floor is best, however, for as you squat over your work, you can bring the whole pressure of your body into the effort. This will make for a darker, more sharply defined print.

Next you will lay the block down on top of the fabric. Center your block in your mind first, so you'll know precisely where it's to go. Once it's down on top of the fabric, that's it—pulling the block off and putting it in another position would ruin the fabric with smeared ink. After positioning the block on the cloth, put your hand on top of the cloth, holding it flush against the block, and turn the whole thing over so the block is now on the floor.

Use a wallpaper roller or an old spoon, and briskly rub over all areas until the ink from each printed portion shows slightly through the cloth.

You can carefully check to see if the cloth is completely printed by lifting the cloth up at one end. Don't pull the whole thing off at once; just peek gingerly under one section at a time. If any spots need more ink, replace the fabric and continue to rub.

When you're finished, slowly remove the cloth, and let the ink dry throughly. The drying may take one or two days, but it can be hastened by outside drying, only watch out for rain. I once left a batik out overnight to find in the morning that a thunderstorm had gotten to it first.

Printing Outlines

The following technique is a great way to combine printing, hand-painting, and batik. Carve out your wood or linoleum block, leaving only those raised areas that are to print the outline of your picture. You could print these in black ink for contrast if you like. After the ink dries you can go back, filling in "inside" the outlines with textile paints or any of the other substances mentioned in the last chapter. This is much like filling in the pages of coloring books as you did when you were a child. Finally you can wax over the entire area, crush the fabric and dye to add crackle or background color.

Printing Wax

Another technique to try is dripping hot wax on either a linoleum or wood block. You can drip any way you want—from abstract primitive blobs to intricate latticework designs. Then ink your brayer and run it over the hardened drippings. You must really use pressure to get the ink into every nook and cranny, especially if some wax blobs are higher than others. Then print, dry, and wax as usual. If you clean the waxed block with turpentine, you can scrape off the wax and then recycle it.

John Peryent and his Wife Joan, *a brass rubbing by Richard J. Busby taken at St. John's Church, Digswell, Herfordshire.*

10
WAX RUBBING BATIK

This method of batiking is another quick way of producing remarkably detailed works of art. Wax rubbings can be made from practically anything that is three-dimensional and has protruding surfaces. It's similar to relief printing batik, only here the work of carving is already done for you. All you have to do is "wax," not print, from the surface of your choice.

The same technique was used in elementary school—you rubbed charcoal over a paper towel that had been placed over radiator grillwork, mesh screening, or any other interesting surface texture. After a few minutes of rubbing, the pressure of the charcoal stick translates the design onto the paper.

These same things hold true for a batik rubbing, except that you use wax for the rubbing medium instead of charcoal. The best fabric to use is fairly thin cotton or muslin. If the fabric is too thick, the pattern simply won't come through no matter how hard you rub. You can use batik wax, or any of the other waxes already mentioned, as well as a candle or crayon.

Medieval Tomb Rubbings

Marvelous rubbings have been done from medieval brass tomb carvings. These carvings can be found in various church graveyards throughout England. If

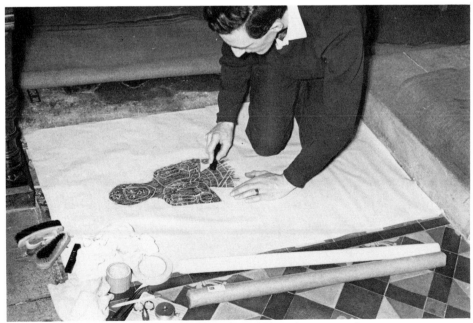

Richard J. Busby in the midst of taking the rubbing shown opposite.

you're interested in an ambitious undertaking, there are special tours you can take of these church sites for the express purpose of making rubbings. In fact these tours have become so popular, they're usually booked solid.

Most traditional rubbings, especially those of the highest quality, are done with paper and prepared black graphite markers. The technique is the same as that used in schools, only it's a bit more sophisticated.

If you're not planning to journey to England, try a museum or local church-yard for elaborate carvings; that is if you want to reproduce real works of art. If, on the other hand, you prefer simplicity, then go to the everyday objects around your house and let your imagination run wild.

Procedure

First place your fabric on top of the object you've chosen to rub from. Tape down the sides of the fabric with masking tape so it can't slide around. Take a candle or a light-colored crayon and rub over the whole area. You should rub quite hard to insure an adequate image. To make sure all the necessary areas have been covered with wax, hold the cloth up to a light. If necessary, go back and rub again to reinforce the wax impression, either over the whole image or just specific areas.

Next put the whole thing in a dye bath, just as you did in the traditional method. It's best to use a fairly dark color for contrast. More details will show up, especially if you use black dye. You could also roll on thickened dye or textile paints as you did for block-printing batik.

You can dye again if you want crackle in the design area. Wax over the whole cloth (or just the previously unwaxed places), crush the fabric, and put it in one or more dye baths. Remove the wax and press thoroughly. It can also be effective to have a crackle border around the whole piece.

Here are a few examples of household items you can take rubbings from: carvings on furniture, screen doors, combs, radiators, decorative mirror frames or picture frames, jewelry, glassware or dishes with raised borders, floor boards, or anything else that has texture.

Wax Rubbing

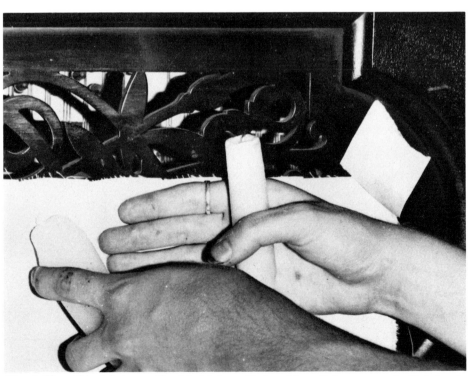

Step 1. *Place thin fabric over the object to be rubbed and tape it down securely. Rub firmly over the whole area with a candle or wax crayon.*

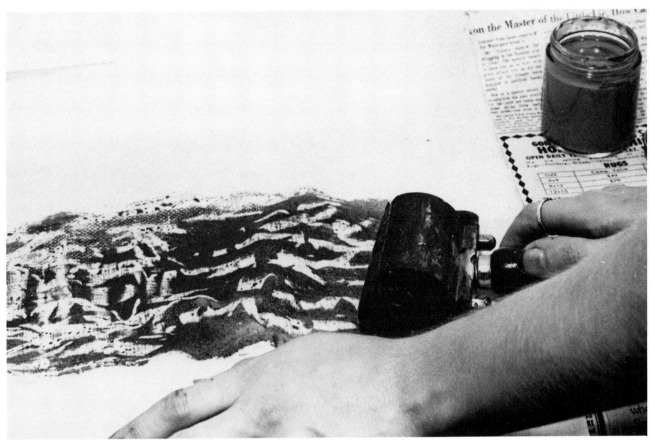

An Alternate Method would be to roll thickened dye on the fabric with a brayer. Press firmly to secure the image of the object you're rubbing.

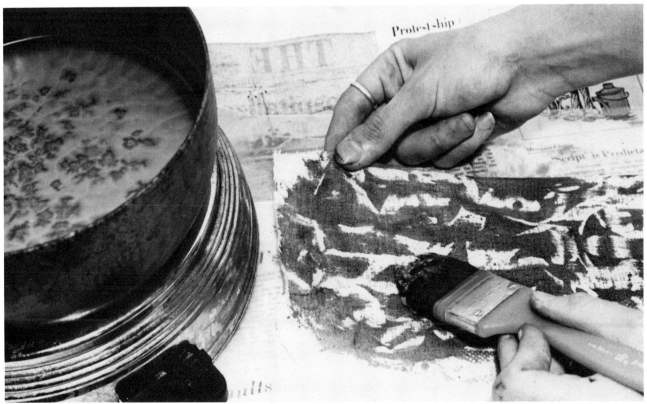

Step 2. Cover the whole fabric with melted wax, crumple the fabric, and submerge in a dye bath.

Contemplation by Mari Eagerton. A fine example of batik portraiture, the artist demonstrates that dyes and wax are quite as capable as paints in creating astounding results.

11
PRINTING FROM NATURAL AND SYNTHETIC OBJECTS

This chapter is really just another branch of the relief printing discussed so far. There are so many different objects, both natural and man-made, that can be utilized for our purposes. This wide range of objects confounds the mind, but at the same time sparks the creative imagination.

Metals

All metals are natural heat conductors (that's why the tjanting tool of traditional batik has a metal cup). Because of this property they can be used to "print" hot wax on cloth.

Check in your tool chest, basement, garage, or lumberyard and you're bound to come up with some goodies. Any intriguing screws, nails, or other metal odds and ends that have a flat surface can be attached to a wooden handle, dipped into hot wax, then printed.

Nails can be knocked into wood with a hammer, or pins can be stuck into a cork. Then wooden handles can be attached for easy printing.

Copper sheets can be cut into shapes. Aluminum foil, which is a metal by-product, can be folded over several times, molded into layers, crunched into balls, or formed into various shapes. Cookie cutters, usually made of tin, are also ideal for wax dipping.

Heat up the metal (including the foil) over a flame to get it good and hot, so it will hold the molten wax. Use the metal just like a rubber stamp. When printing, stamp only one or two impressions of each object. Any more than that and the print will get hazy and the wax will be too weak to "resist" the dye's action.

Synthetics

Styrofoam can be cut into shapes and dipped in wax. Cardboard is also useful. You can cut it into simple shapes such as stars, hearts, moons, or flowers. Try cutting up small sections of paper towel tubing, egg cartons, or boxes, and tape them together to form more interesting shapes. Handles can be put on these constructions by bending wire, attaching it in the center, and twisting to hold.

Pieces of felt fabric can be cut into shapes and pasted down (or nailed) to wood. Pipe cleaners bend easily and will take on almost any shape you want with a little maneuvering. Use long ones so that after your shape is made, you'll have enough pipe cleaner left over to form its own handle. These can be purchased in thin form or the extra-large almost furry looking ones. They can be used separately or combined into a motley pattern.

Printing Objects (*Above*). *Here are some of the everyday items that can be used to print wax on fabric.*

A Fish Print *is both fun to make and visually dramatic. First wipe all the oil off the fish or the wax won't adhere, then coat a roller with ink, and print.*

Natural Objects

Many natural objects such as feathers, leaves, ferns, or pressed flowers can be printed by rolling over them gently with an ink-filled brayer. The same holds true for fish, believe it or not. Visit a fish market and select one that has striking scales. You don't even have to hold your nose when you're printing, because the ink's smell will outdo the fish's. Run the brayer lightly over the scales. Don't use too much ink or some of the delicate details will be lost. You can even print your hands, feet, or any other part of your anatomy for surrealistic effects.

Printing Hints

All of the printing objects just mentioned can either be printed singly or combined to produce intriguing repeat patterns. This repeat printing may cause some of the pipe cleaners and cardboard pieces to lose their shape. Just remake them if this happens.

Whenever you stamp your fabric with a wax stamper, make sure the cloth is on a stable surface with wax paper underneath to catch any drips.

Making a "Stamp Pad"

When dipping pipe cleaners or other things into wax, it's helpful to place a foam-rubber stamper in the bottom of your wax pan (use a pan with shallow sides to facilitate dipping). This will act as a firm surface from which to gather wax, thus

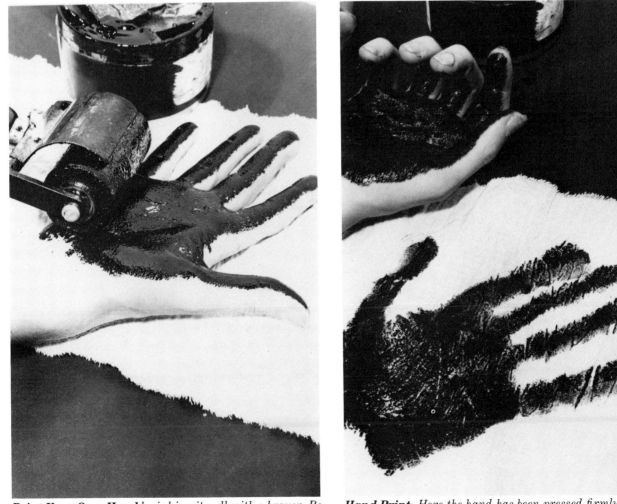

Print Your Own Hand by inking it well with a brayer. Be sure there is no grease on your palm or the ink will not stick.

Hand Print. Here the hand has been pressed firmly to the fabric.

Making a Stamper

Step 1. *Put a small piece of foam rubber in a small saucepan and put the stamper on top of it (in this case a formed pipe cleaner).*

Step 2. *Pour wax into the pan until it just covers the top of the pad.*

hastening the dipping process. Have just enough wax in the pan to cover the top of the foam rubber (this way the pad won't float around).

Stamp the object you're printing with down on the foam-rubber pad. Press firmly so it will pick up enough wax to saturate its surface. This way you'll get an evenly printed image. After printing, you may need to go back over your designs with wax to reinforce the first waxing.

One final word—never throw anything out without first examining its creative potential. What first appears to be a piece of garbage could well be a gold mine in disguise.

Step 3. *Apply the waxed stamper to your fabric.*

Enchanted Bird *by Mari Eagerton. Here is a charming example of a stuffed batik. The fabric was waxed and dyed, then cut out and stuffed.*

12
OTHER RESISTS

In addition to hot wax, there are many other resists that can be used for batik. Cold wax, flour paste, and masking tape can all be used, either by themselves or together with hot wax. They all perform the same service of isolating areas of fabric until they have been dyed.

Cold Wax

This wax works on the same principle as hot wax, except its chemical components are slightly different. You don't have to mix it, or wait for the wax to melt. All you do is apply it right from the jar. You can even dilute it with water for a thinner solution. Brush it on, squirt it out from a squeeze bottle, or roll it on with a brayer. You can also apply it with your fingers, provided it hasn't had time to harden. Another great feature is that once it's on, you can easily remove it from the fabric if you want to change its position. It's best to do this while the wax is still damp by rubbing firmly with a cloth or towel. If the wax has already dried, you can scrape it off with a dull knife. You can even scratch designs into the wax with nails, or wire before dyeing for interesting visual effects. One disadvantage of cold wax is that you must wait for the wax to harden before applying the color. This takes about an hour. It may, however, take a little more or a bit less time, depending on the brand you use. When it's completely dry, crush it just as you did with the cooled, hot wax. The cold wax will crack, and after you apply color you will have those veinlike lines so characteristic of batiks.

For different colors, continue waxing and dyeing until you're satisfied with the results. You can immerse the fabric in a dye bath, because the wax isn't water-soluble and won't wash out. You can also use fabric paints. To remove cold wax use any of the methods discussed in Chapter 2.

Cold wax will save you the headache of controlling wax temperatures, but *because the wax isn't hot—it won't penetrate through the fabric*. To compensate for this, you'll have to wax the back of your batik separately if you don't want the dye from the back to show through to the front. This won't matter so much if you're working with light dyes, but the darker or stronger colors will overwhelm any delicate tones you want to keep.

Flour Paste

You can make a solution of flour and water and apply it to cloth in the same way that you applied the cold wax. But it's important to remember that you can't submerge flour-coated fabrics in water because the flour will dissolve. Be careful not to forget this point, or the whole batik will go down the drain—literally!

To make the flour paste, add 3 or 4 teaspoons of flour to 1 cup of water. The

Tape and Flour Paste

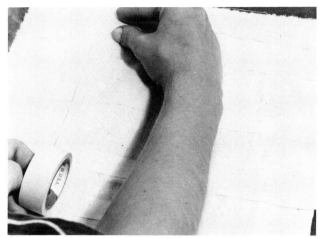

Step 1. Put masking tape on the fabric according to the desired design.

Step 2. Mix the flour and water (approximately 3 or 4 tsps. of flour to each cup of water) and stir well. Heat the mixture, still stirring, until the surface becomes glossy.

Step 3. Apply the flour paste to all areas of the cloth with a soft brush and let dry.

Step 4. Pull off the tape and color the exposed areas with dyes or textile paints.

Step 5. Wash the flour paste off the fabric. Then you can wax and dye for crackle.

Fabric Resisting. Here the fabric is actually resiting itself. Hot wax is brushed on one side of thin folded cloth, and it will penetrate through the layers.

Jungle King *by Joanifer. This bold beast is an example of discharge dyeing.*

Space Divider *by Jennifer F. Lew, 6½ x 6 feet. This detail shows how easily batik can be combined with other textures, in this case lengths of jute.*

amount of water will vary according to the desired spreading consistency.

Next heat the mixture, using either a double-boiler or a single pan. Heat it for several minutes until the top surface gets glossy. Stir frequently to dissolve any lumps.

This same method has been and is still practiced in Nigeria and Java, where the people use a thick starch called Cassava to protect the cloth from the dyes.

Apply the paste to the cloth with a brush. Put it on thickly, so it covers all areas thoroughly. Wait 24 hours or overnight for the flour to get bone dry before coloring. Coat the fabric with color—either dye or pigment—and allow the fabric to dry. Then wash out the flour paste resist.

Masking Tape

Ordinary masking tape may be attached to cloth in many different patterns and shapes, just by sticking it down firmly. It can be purchased in thin and thick strips. These can alternately be combined to make striking geometric designs.

Put down the tape and apply a resist (any one you like) to the un-taped areas of the fabric. Be careful if you're using hot wax—don't overlap the tape itself or the wax will burn through. Also the tape will be harder to remove if heat affects it. Also, don't ever submerge the fabric in a dye bath or liquid of any type while tape is on it or it will wash off. Pull off the tape and paint or dye the previously masked areas. As with the other techniques, you can then wax and redye if you want crackle.

Fabric Resisting

An interesting technique to try is to let fabric resist itself. Fold the fabric in half, making sure the fabric is thin. Wax both sides of the fabric, and the heat will penetrate them both for equal resistance. Then unfold and dye.

Bleach or Discharge Dyeing

This technique of color control has the opposite effect of the other methods we've discussed—color is taken away (or subtracted) instead of added. Wax resist is still used, but it is applied to a dark shade of cloth, cracked, and submerged in bleach, not a dye bath. This removes all, or at least some, of the fabric color, depending on how long the cloth is left in the solution. Rinse out all of the bleach afterward, and remove the wax.

Mandala *by Jennifer F. Lew. This batik hanging suggests the formations found in flowers, where petals and seeds cluster around the central pistil.*

13

BATIKING ON PAPER

Any batik process discussed so far can be used on paper. The results won't be as permanent, however, because paper isn't as long-lasting as cloth. One big advantage is that paper is inexpensive, so it's good to use for children's school projects that don't need to hold up for a long period of time.

Types of Paper

You've got to use strong papers with sturdy fibers to withstand handling and dye-bath submergings. Bond, heavy drawing, and watercolor paper, as well as the thicker Japanese brands, will do a fine job. You might try using various colors and textures too, for variety.

Resists

Hot and cold waxes, flour paste, masking tape, rubber cement and stencils can all be used on paper. They produce wonderful results if used wisely. By "wisely" I mean remembering the general rules for each process. For example, not putting a tape or flour "in progress" batik into a tub full of water. This would result in disaster.

Dyes and Pigments

Any type of dye or pigment will do, since paper accepts all color readily and permanency is not as much of a factor. You should still use thickened dyes and color-fast pigments if you want the color to withstand several dye submersions.

Procedure

Here, step by step, is the process of batiking on paper:

Preparing the Paper. Wet the paper gently all over before you begin. This is not absolutely essential, but it will produce soft, delicate dyeing. This particular look goes especially well with Oriental papers such as mulberry or rice. Next stretch the paper. Do this while it's still damp and still has enough "give." To stretch, tack the paper to a box top, board, or stretcher. As you tack, pull each section slightly towards you. Be gentle though or the paper might tear. This step will prevent any shrinkage later on.

The Resist. Use any resist you want, for example, cold wax or flour are fine. They all accomplish the same thing. Cover all areas where you don't want color.

Coloring. Use either thickened dyes or the color-fast pigments that we just discussed. The paper can go through several colorings just like regular batik.

Batiking On Paper

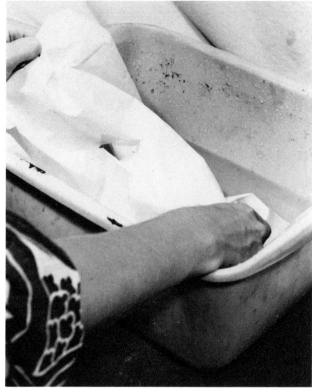

Step 1. *Wet the paper thoroughly in a tub of water.*

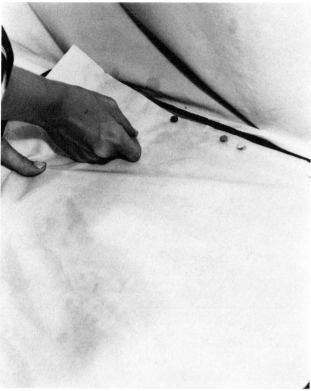

Step 2. *Carefully stretch the wet paper by tacking the edges to a canvas stretcher or cardboard box.*

Step 3. *Draw the design, then wax the paper with cold wax and a brush.*

Step 4. *Add the desired color to the unwaxed portions.*

Step 5. *Brush cold wax over the surface of the paper, crush carefully, and apply more color if you want crackle. Then remove the resist.*

Crackle. If you want crackle, brush cold wax over any areas that haven't yet received wax, or over the whole piece. Crush the paper, and go through the usual coloring steps.

Remove the Resist. The method you choose will depend on which resist you picked in the first place. For example, if you used regular "hot" wax, then you'd use an iron; whereas for flour paste you would have to use water. If you wash out the resist, then iron the paper on both the back and the front to set the color.

Final Touches. Afterwards, a good way to give a paper batik that extra zap is to varnish it by coating the whole design with vegetable oil. You can use regular floor varnish, but it tends to be really smelly. Just apply two coats of cooking oil lightly over your colors, and a soft glow will flow outwards. This will look especially brilliant when held up to a light.

Because paper sometimes falls apart after much handling, you can expect some failures. Any of these can be saved in part, if not in whole. Pick the best parts of several failures and combine these into a collage along with any other odds and ends you might have lying about. Old newspaper or magazine pictures, fabric remnants, yarn, string, buttons, or any other objects that happen to catch your eye are all possibilities. Some truly unique pieces can result from just the "right" combination of things.

Kitchen Wall Hanging *by Lillian Donald, 78″ x 108″. This detail of a large tie-dyed piece shows the skill and control necessary to produce the vibrational, textural tone. It is shown in color on p. 71.*

14

TIE-DYED FABRIC

Batik and tie-dye are two sides of the same coin—they're both "resist" processes. In the tie-dyeing process, however, simple string acts as the resist. By tying the string tightly around fabric and folding the cloth in various ways, many exciting patterns can be achieved. Any of the materials used for batik can also be used for tie-dyeing. Also, I've found that Japanese papers as well as fabric can be folded and dyed with equally rewarding results.

Handling Cloth

There are many ways you can handle fabric before submerging it in the dye baths. You may want to experiment by trying out these different methods on old sheeting or inexpensive material remnants. These methods are simple, but they can be elaborated upon singly or in combination, so that their variations become endless. Each individual craftsman has to decide for himself which way of tying or which type of fold he likes best.

The Basic Technique

Circular, angular, geometric, and motley patterns can all be achieved by positioning the ties and the fabric in various ways. Experiment by twisting and knotting the material before tying. If you prefer uncomplicated, pristine designs, then you don't have to contort the cloth. Merely tie it in clusters, either loosely or tightly bunched together.

First position the fabric, then tie the decided areas. You can use string, ribbon, rope, cord, or rubber bands. These ties can be knotted several times to hold fast or you can wrap several layers of string around and around to further block the dye's action. Don't tie too tightly, however, or it will be impossible to undo your efforts.

Dyeing. Dump the cloth into your dye bath. Fabrics can remain in the dye baths for as long as desired, depending on the intensity of color that's required. Just as with batik, the fabric should be dyed in a container that's large enough for it to move about freely and to be completely covered with dye. This will insure even, no-streak dyeing. A mordant can be added to the dye bath to help set the color. It's not necessary to watch out for hot dyes, as was necessary with batik (unless you're combining the two processes). When only working with tie-dye, it's perfectly fine to use any dye temperature you want because there's no melting wax to worry about.

Untying the Fabric. After dyeing, the ties can be cut with scissors or a sharp knife. Make sure you exercise care when cutting so the fabric won't be damaged in any way.

Tying Arrangements

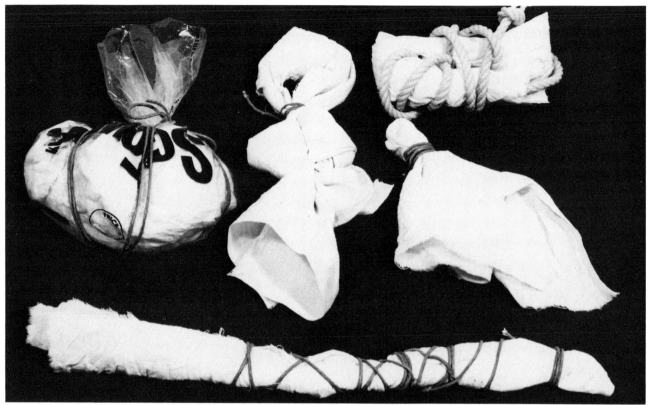

1. *These pieces of unbleached muslin have been tied with rope or heavy cord. One has been placed in a plastic bag prior to tying. Holes are then punched in the bag to allow dye to seep into those areas.*

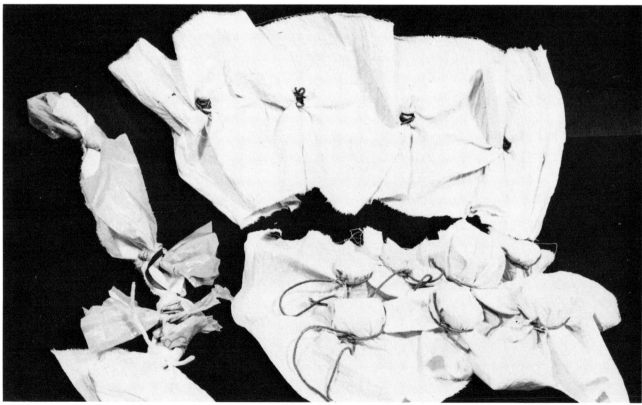

2. *Here fabric has been tied with jute, bunched with rubber bands, and fastened with pipe cleaners and covered wire. One piece was tied with strips cut from a plastic bag; another has marbles tied inside to create a circular composition.*

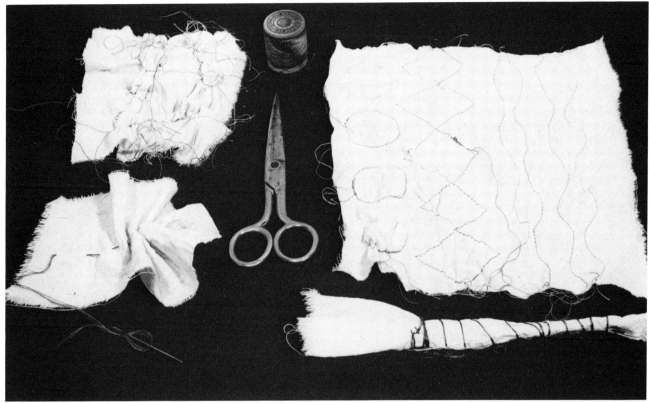

3. The fabrics shown here have been hand gathered or machine stitched, adding yet more tie-dye dimensions.

4. Fabric clamped between two pieces of wood is another effective resist.

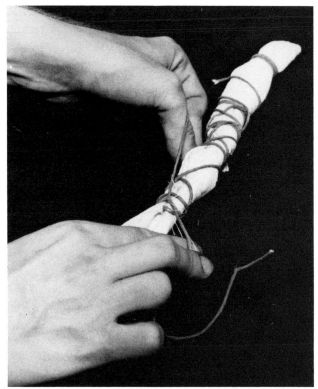

Step 1. *Tie up the fabric in any way you want.*

Step 2. *Put the fabric in a dye bath until the desired color is reached, then let it dry thoroughly.*

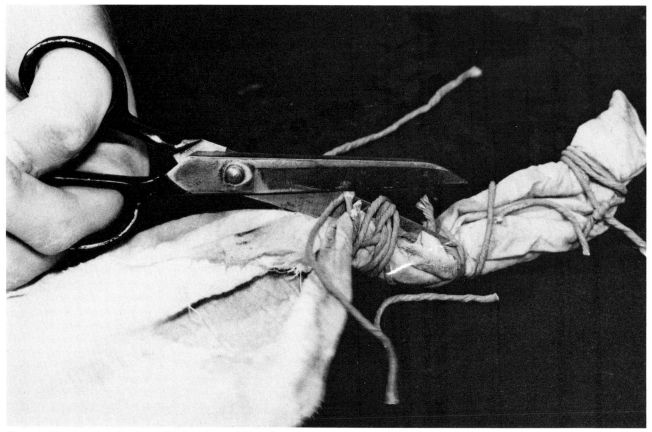

Step 3. *Remove the ties from the fabric, and then iron to remove any wrinkles.*

Folding and Pleating

Folds and pleats can be used in many interesting ways. Once a fabric or paper is folded, it doesn't have to be tied to hold its form. It can be dipped directly into the dye or have dye dripped or painted on it in certain sections only. Accordion pleats are fun, but make sure the fabric is fairly thin or else folding will be difficult and the dye will have trouble penetrating the cloth. Before folding or pleating any actual fabric, try out some tests on paper. Paper is much easier to work with at first, and when you've become familiar with a special fold, then you can translate it to fabric.

Stitching and Gathering

Fabric can be gathered and stitched by using heavy thread to hold the sections of cloth together. This thread should be fairly strong, so it will hold fast without breaking. Use a long thread, knotted at one end, and pull this through as many layers of folds or pleats as you want. You can gather certain parts close together, or spread out to cover a large area. After you've finished, pull the thread taut and you'll find that these folds will be held by the thread. These will stay stationary if you carefully tie both ends of the string together before dyeing.

Clamping

Ties and thread alone resist only small portions of cloth unless their forces are multiplied, but it's good to know that you can resist larger areas if you wish. Get two pieces of thin plywood of any size and shape, and place the fabric between them. Small C-clamps can serve to hold the plywood around the cloth. Attach them to both sides of the wood if you want the whole area underneath to resist dye. You can also cut the plywood into many shapes with an electric saw for more variations.

Tying Up Objects

The last method we'll look at is placing various objects inside bunched up fabric. If you're using more than one item, first tie them together with rubber bands or string. Next they are tied up in the actual fabric by knotting or stringing. When they're in place, they'll resist the dye. Any object that strikes your fancy can be used. Of course the more unusual the object is, the stranger your imprint will be. Never tie in anything you value, or the dye is sure to ruin it. Also use lighter-weight objects, so the cloth won't tear. Styrofoam forms can be used, although they may permit a little dye to seep into places you don't expect. Tennis balls, plastic bottles, and pencils all make intriguing patterns

Tie-Dye and Batik

The combination of tie-dye and batik is very appealing. After you've completed your batik you can tie-dye certain parts, or vice-versa. The fabric can either be dumped into a dye bath or dyed proportionally, section by section, in one or more dye baths. Certain sections can be isolated and dyed again with different colors, or the same section may be folded or tied again and redyed for multiple colorations and designs.

Miracle Woman by Moraq Benepe. This stuffed batik is an example of fun-fantasy at its best. Courtesy of the American Crafts Council, New York.

15
COMBINING MEDIA, AND ANYTHING GOES

Right now, the craft of batik is expanding to include other forms of expression. It is becoming more and more accepted to combine one medium with another, as long as the craftsman gets satisfying results. For example, aside from just using the techniques we've discussed separately or in combination, it's perfectly valid to bring other crafts or objects into the picture. Truly exciting effects can be achieved by using a little bit of ingenuity.

Natural Objects

Glorious wall hangings can be made by combining natural objects with batiks. For instance, dried wildflowers, leaves, ferns, or bird feathers (peacock feathers are exceptionally lovely) can be glued or sewn onto portions of your batik. To preserve this fine craftsmanship, it's best to cover the fabric with some type of protection. Regular plate glass or plexiglass and a picture frame are recommended.

Egg shells—either natural or dyed—can be broken into small pieces and glued on fabrics. Tiny sea shells can also be attached to cloth by punching a hole in the shell and sewing it on. Sand and very small pebbles can be used as well. Spray or brush glue lightly on the fabric before throwing on the sand. The pebbles will need more glue to hold them in place. Many seeds and beans, such as pumpkin, apple, and watermelon seeds, or kidney beans, can also be glued to your fabric, providing exciting mosaic effects. If you want to attach heavy or bulky objects to your cloth, it should be backed-up. This can be done either with wood or heavy cardboard. *Note:* if you use wood for it your back-up your objects on the fabric *before* gluing it to the wood. If thinner cardboard is employed, you can sew the objects right through the batik and the cardboard. If you back your cloth on wood, fold the excess fabric over the sides and tack it; if you use cardboard either tape or glue the excess fabric to the back to form a finished, even edge.

Other Ideas

Another idea is to glue or sew beads to your batik. Beads come in various sizes and materials, ranging from the tiny, multicolored glass Indian beads to the large hand-carved wooden kind. These can be particularily attractive if combined in an artistic way. Batik can also be combined with ceramic or papier mâché forms for lovely results. Colored Japanese tissue paper looks enchanting if sewn or pasted on batiked paper or cloth. Broken bits of mirror or stained glass can be glued also, but the cloth must be attached firmly to a backing of some sort.

Any type of stitchery combines exceptionally well with batik—it provides that natural "homespun" look. You can put embroidery, crewel, or needlepoint

Combined Media Batik

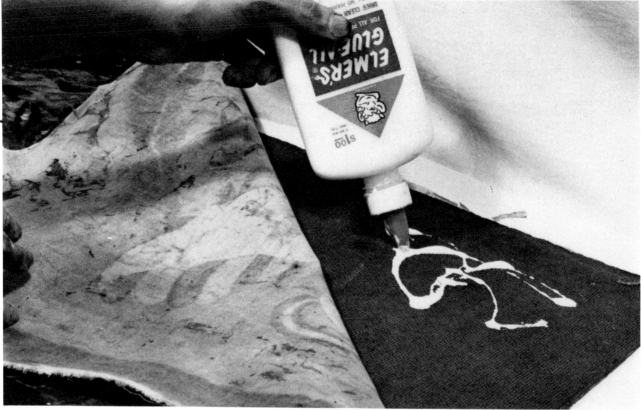

Step 1. *Glue a finished batik to a Masonite board.*

Step 2. *Glue on lentil beans and seeds.*

stitches right on top of your batik. Macramé and weaving are also attractive if sewn onto batiked cloth. Rows of smooth satin square knots are lightweight and can be attached to the top of a batik so they'll hang down freely. Pieces of yarn or string can be dipped in clear glue and adhered to the cloth in many intriguing patterns.

All the things I've mentioned so far have involved building materials around the central theme of a batik painting. However, it's possible to reverse this procedure and start adding batik fabrics to enhance other structures. For example, suppose you have a plain woven hanging. Even though this hanging may have some type of decoration such as bells, twigs, or feathers, it may still seem drab without a touch of color. If you think color is needed to brighten things up, you could cut an old batik into strips, sew up the raveled edges, and attach them to the hanging in a decorative way.

Overworking a Design

Unfortunately, all the ideas in this book can easily be overdone. A batik can become confusing to the eye if you combine everything you've learned in the same piece. For example, mixing shells, mirrors, and macramé together would probably be *too* much. This is why it's so important to know where to stop. With so many creative options open, it's really hard to pick the one or ones that will best suit your work. In any pictorial representation or straight design concept, it's often better to take away elements or simplify, rather than add extraneous material. Simplicity has value in and of itself. In other words, a batik may look terrific in its own right—without any other devices; on the other hand, just a touch of beading or some other material may complement and enrich the entire feeling or mood of the picture.

Step 3. *Now glue on shells and spaghetti sticks to complete the decorative effects.*

Batiking Eggs

One really different thing I haven't mentioned so far is batiking eggs. Batiked eggs are popular during holiday seasons: at Christmas they can be seen hanging from trees, Easter finds them gracing tables as a symbol of spring's rebirth. These eggs, called *pysanka*, were first made by Ukraine artists who saw that hot wax could be applied effectively as a resist to an egg's surface. Eggs can be decorated with geometric designs, plant and animal motifs, or a combination of both. The traditional eggs are quite often symbolic in their decorations. For example, the star and cross are taken from the iconography of the early Christian Church.

See the demonstration nearby for the step-by-step process in the creation of a pysanka, or decorated egg. This particular egg will be four colors—white, yellow, red, and black.

I prefer to use a raw egg for batiking because it's easier to work with. You could also empty the egg or hard-boil it, and these procedures are described at the end of this section. This egg should be unwashed, but clean and preferably right from the farm, or as fresh as possible. The shape is very important, too. It should be oval, never pointed. Divide the egg into sections by either putting a rubber band lengthwise around the egg, or by sketching a dividing line freehand. To do this, use either a *kistka* (a Ukrainian writing tool), a tjanting, or a brush to apply the wax. Handle with care, the egg will break if dropped!

Draw your design lightly on the egg with pencil. Wax only those areas where you want white or the original color of the egg to remain. Dye the egg in the lightest color (yellow). Use either an egg dipper or a spoon to hold the egg while you dye. Keep the egg immersed until the desired color is reached.

Next wax the places to stay yellow. Make sure the egg is completely dry before waxing or the wax won't adhere. Use a cloth or tissue to wipe off excess moisture. Continue the dyeing process until all the colors have been used.

To remove the wax, light some sterno, which is canned cooking fuel, and rotate the egg directly on top of the flame until all the wax melts away. Use a cloth to catch the excess. Wipe well all over until all the wax is removed.

The last step is to coat the egg with varnish. Use clear varnish and coat lightly twice. If you used a raw egg this will seal off the pores so air can't get in to rot it out. When firmly sealed off the egg will decompose gradually over the years without smelling.

Other Ways of Dyeing. As you have seen, this egg-decorating process is almost identical to the "traditional" batik in every respect. There are, however, other ways to dye eggs. You can paint dyes directly onto the egg and you can also paint on melted wax as you did for crayon batik.

Preserving Old Eggs. Some eggs become especially fragile after the contents dry up. To keep them from breaking, it's a good idea to make a small hole at one end with a sharp needle and fill the inside with hot wax. When this hardens, it will give the egg added weight for a longer life.

Note. You may prefer to drain out the contents of the egg before dyeing. Use a sharp needle to make a hole at either end and blow out the inside liquid. These eggs are very fragile to work with, and an alternative is to hard-boil them. Either of these two methods may be used if you don't like working with a raw egg. Later, you can fill the empty egg with wax. The hard-boiled one can be filled too when the insides deteriorate. You won't find a better preservative than this "wax-filling."

Silkscreen Batik

Another process you can try is to silkscreen a batik. This is another printing procedure that can be used in the same way as the block printing process. Construct a frame and stretch a piece of silk across it. Then you can print with silk-

Batiking Eggs

Step 1. *Hold the egg gently but firmly. Divide it into sections according to the desired design.*

Step 2. *Draw the design in wax with a "kistka." It works in the same way as a tjanting, but has a finer point. These waxed parts will stay the original color of the egg.*

Step 3. *Dip the egg in the lightest color dye (yellow) with a spoon or egg dipper.*

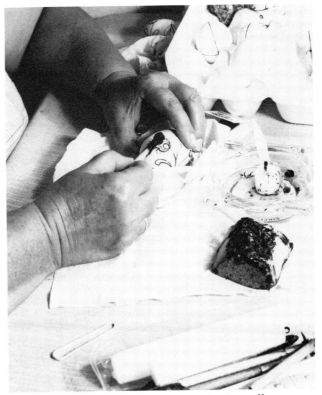

Step 4. *Wax the areas that you want to stay yellow.*

Step 5. *Dip the egg in a medium color dye (red).*

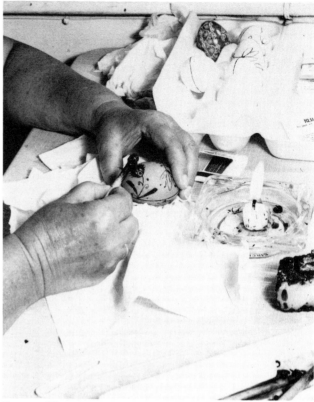

Step 6. *Wax the portions to stay red.*

Step 7. *Dip the egg in the darkest color, black.*

Step 8. *Light a can of sterno and rotate the egg over the flame to remove the wax. Wipe the melting wax off the egg with a cloth.*

Batiked Eggs. *A basket of completed eggs, resplendent with traditional Ukranian motifs.*

Silkscreen Printing. *This photo shows the traditional setup for making a silkscreen.*

screen paint on the surface of the cloth. Apply paint to the top of the frame and rub it across with a squeegee. After the paint dries, wax over the whole printed area, crack the wax, and dye. These are only brief instructions, so see the Bibliography on page 147 for books that offer further information on the silkscreen process.

Stuffed Batik

Today, many craftsmen are starting to break away from flat art and are rapidly moving toward the three-dimensional world. Stuffing batiked cloth with various fillers is a direct outgrowth of this current pattern.

Any batik can potentially be used for a stuffed creation. It's best to plan exactly what kind of form you want, however, so provisions can be made for a sewing pattern. Assuming you've finished the batik you plan to stuff, make sure that you have an identically-sized piece of either batiked or plain fabric handy for a backing. Then sew the pieces, keeping right sides together. Leave a space to turn the fabric right side out. Next, carefully fill the form with either polyester filler, cotton, or rubber foam, and sew up the cloth's opening so no stuffing will fall out. These fillers can be purchased at most department stores, sewing or notions stores, or at many five-and-dimes.

Blue Lady by Moraq Benepe. A whimsical stuffed figure. Courtesy of the American Crafts Council, New York.

Icarus *by Moraq Benepe. Another fantastic stuffed batik. The wings, in keeping with the Greek myth, do seem to be melting. Courtesy of the American Crafts Council, New York.*

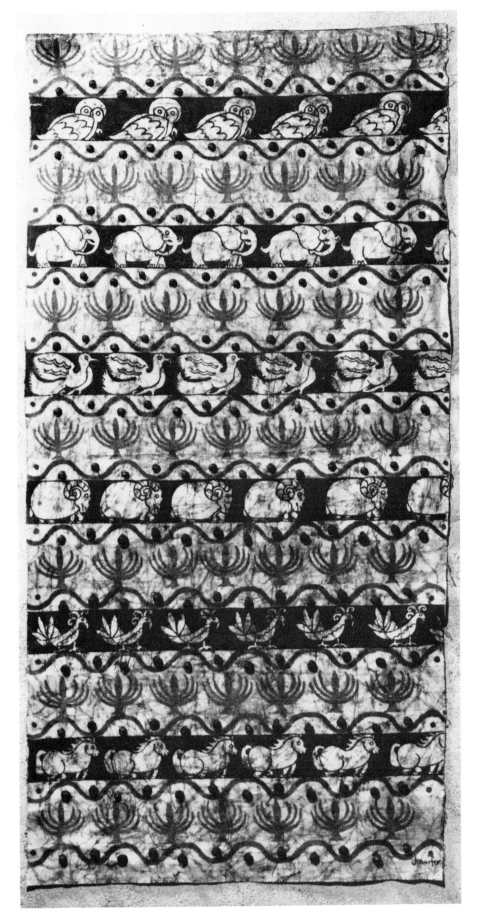

Animal Processions *by Joanifer.*
Black bugle beads were sewn on this
batik to give it a three-dimensional
quality.

Landscape I by Andra Frank. This stuffed batik uses wood for inside support.

Landscape II *by Andra Frank. Here the stuffed batik has been mounted like a painting.*

Hanging Batiks. *A metal pole run through velvet, a curtain rod with a decorative wood fixture at the end, and wood stripping with the batik inside are just some of the ways to hang your batiks.*

16
FRAMING AND CARE OF COMPLETED WORK

Framing and caring for your finished products is almost as important as their creation. Handle your batiks with great love and they'll respond by lasting out their years.

Most batiked fabrics should be washed by hand, as the washing machine tosses them around too much. Machine-washing is hard on any fabrics, much less hand-crafted pieces. However, if the fabric happens to be very sturdy, then it's okay. This holds true especially for batiked clothes that you plan to wear often, such as sweat shirts, jeans, or shirts. Fine garments, such as elaborate evening gowns, should be dry-cleaned by all means. All batik hangings that you value should also be dry-cleaned. And if the colors you've selected aren't "positively" color-fast you should always dry-clean.

Here are some ways to present your work. Pick the one that seems to add the most to your creation and will show it off to the best advantage.

Stretchers

Buy some artists' canvas stretchers, or make your own from pieces of lumber. Stretch the cloth over the frame and attach it with nails or staples, making sure it's centered and pulled fairly taut. Nail or staple into the back of the wood, not the sides, so they won't show. This way you can hang the batik on the wall without unsightly hardware interfering with the "total" viewing area. If the fabric doesn't have enough surrounding border area to stretch around to the back, then you can staple it to the sides and add wooden stripping to cover. This stripping will also serve as a frame for your work.

You might want to varnish the wood strips or paint them a solid color that matches or accents the batik. Use either flat or enamel paint. Flat paint tends to recede, while enamel or glossy paint stands out. Strips of aluminum siding are also great to use if you want to have a modern, professional look.

Hangings

When you want your batik to hang freely, like a tapestry, it still needs some type of support. Wooden strips of thin, flat pine or balsa wood can be placed at just the top of the batik or at the bottom as well. When these wooden strips are cut to size and stapled to both ends of the fabric, they will enable the batik to hang straight and flush against the wall. For a more finished look, use two strips of wood—one varnished or painted, the other plain—sandwiching the cloth in between. These may be nailed together once the cloth has been inserted but make sure the nails aren't too long or they'll come through the wood. You can allow the wooden strips to extend an inch or so beyond the batik's border or match them up evenly with the cloth's edge.

Velvet Strips *sewn to the top and bottom of this batik create a semi-formal feeling.*

Borders

For a plain batik that has no border other than its own boundaries, here's what you do. Get some special stick-on fabric glue, like the brand called "Jiffy Sew" by Esquire, which is carried at most sewing centers. This comes in a tube and is very easy to apply. In fact it is a life saver. Before I found the glue, I had been laboriously stitching my batiks by hand. This had to be done carefully, so the stitching wouldn't show.

Before using this glue, first measure how much of the batik you want to fold under (usually an inch or so). Hold the fabric against a floor board or other straight edge to line up the fold. Next fold back the cloth against the board's line and apply the glue inside the fold. You won't need too much, just a little squirted right out of the tube will do it. Press the fabric together right away, as the glue dries instantly. Keep rubbing your fingers over the cloth for a minute or two to make sure the material is tacked down to stay.

When the glue has dried thoroughly the fabric can be washed, and the glue won't be affected by the action of the water. What an invention!

If the sides of your material have a selvage, or woven edge, then you won't need to turn the edges under. The main reason for turning is to keep the fibers from unraveling at a later date.

Unfishished. *This batik has been left plain, without any decorative additions.*

Medieval Finishing. *Strips of velvet have been sewn all around, and muslin and velvet flaps at the bottom complete the finishing.*

Wooden Stripping *is perfect to complete a batik that is modern in feeling.*

Floral Arrangement *by Dorothy Cecil, 21″ x 24″. Here a batik has been surrounded by a mat cut from heavy white mat-board. Clear acetate protects the front, and heavy cardboard the back.*

Fabric Borders

For a rich, medieval tapestry look, velvet is a good choice for a border. For a more rustic, homemade look, burlap has charm. Actually any material can be used for a border, depending on the style of your batik.

To make a border at the top and bottom of a batik, cut your fabric into two strips. Four strips are cut out if you want to border all four sides. Make sure these strips are all equal in size if you plan to frame the work. Another method is to run a pole, either wood or metal, through the fabric for hanging. Then you've got to plan on about two or three inches of extra cloth at the top to turn over so the pole can slide through.

With right sides of the fabrics together, pin the border sections, one at a time, to the batik and sew. A sewing machine is recommended, as it's much faster than handstitching. If you're using a pole, make sure the openings are wide enough to permit the pole to slide through easily. You can tie cord, or ribbon to both ends of the rod to facilitate hanging, or attach metal holders to the wall for the poles to rest on. A second pole can be run through the bottom of the hanging to distribute the weight further. For large batiks this is very helpful.

Backing

When hanging a large piece of work you may find that the cloth will buckle. Fabrics tend to do this if they're thin or excessively lengthy. The only solution is to back these fabrics with another type of material (cotton or felt). Often these don't come sized to exactly fit your batik, so you'll have to piece the backing together. Then pin, right sides together, to the batik and sew around three sides. Leave the fourth side unsewn so you can turn the whole thing inside out, then sew it up. Iron both the "joined" fabrics well to remove any wrinkles that might have appeared.

Framing

Sometimes it's wise to protect your batik within an actual picture frame. This method of display serves not only as protection, but also as decoration. Both elaborate and simple frames can be purchased at a framing store or found at antique shops, garage sales, or junkyards. Old, seemingly battered Victorian frames can be refinished to look like new with a little elbow grease. Another idea is to sandwich your batik between two pieces of plexiglass. Hanging attachments of metal and string can be fastened to the sides with clip-on holders. Plexiglass is hard to break, which is a relief to anyone who has ever smashed a newly framed picture's glass by mistake! You do have to watch out for scratches with plastics, but they're not too hard to avoid once the picture is hanging on the wall. You'll find that this new type of "chemical glass" will lend an uncluttered, streamlined look to any work of art.

BIBLIOGRAPHY

Bystrom, Ellen. *Printing On Fabrics*. New York: Van Nostrand Reinhold Company, 1967

Collier, Graham. *Form, Space, and Vision*. New Jersey: Prentice-Hall Inc., 1963

Deyrup, Astrith. *Getting Started in Batik*. New York: Bruce Publishing Company, 1971

Hess, Katherine P. *Textile Fibers and Their Use*. New York: J.B. Lippincott Company, 1958

Hunt, Anthony. *Textile Design*. New York: Studio Publications Inc., 1937

Jameson, Norma. *Batik for Beginners*. New York: Watson-Guptill, 1970. London: Studio Vista, 1970

Keller, Ira. *Batik: the Art and Craft*. Vermont: Charles E. Tuttle Company, 1966

Kosloff, Albert. *Textile Screen Printing*. Cincinnati, Ohio: Signs of the Times Publishing Company, 1966

Lesch, Alma. *Vegetable Dyeing*. New York: Watson-Guptill Publications, 1970

Leechman, Douglas. *Vegetable Dyes from North American Plants*. Toronto, Canada: Oxford University Press, 1945

Monk, Kathlene. *The Craft of Fabric Printing*. New York: Ballantine Books, 1969

Nea, Sara. *Batik*. New York and London: Van Nostrand Reinhold Company, 1970

Ocvirk, Otto; Bone, Robert; Stinson, Robert; Wigg, Philip. *Art Fundamentals, Theory and Practice*. Iowa: William C. Brown Company, Inc., 1974

Proud, Nora. *Textile Printing and Dyeing*. New York: Van Nostrand Reinhold Company, 1965

Rice, Stanley. *Getting Started in Prints and Patterns*. New York: Bruce Publishing Company, 1971

Stribling, Mary Lou. *Art from Found Materials*. New York: Crown Publishers Inc., 1971

Watson, William. *Textile Design and Color*. New York: Longmans, Green and Company, 1954

SUPPLIERS LIST

DYES

Aljo Manufacturing Company, Inc.
116 Prince Street
New York, New York 10012

American Hoechst Corp.
Main Office
129 Quidnick Street
Coventry, Rhode Island 02816

Craftool Batik Dyes
Wood-Ridge, New Jersey 07075

Cushing & Co.,
Dover Foxcroft, Maine 04426

Dylon International Ltd.
139-151 Sydenham Road
London, S.E. 26, England

Empire-White Products Co.
45 Herman Street
Newark, New Jersey 07108

Fabdec
P.O. Box 3060
Lubbock, Texas 79410

Farquhar Fabric Dyes
6 Clarence Square
Toronto 135, Ontario, Canada

Fezandie & Sperrle, Inc.
103 Lafayette Street
New York, New York 10013

Fibrec
2795 16th Street
San Francisco, California 94103

Keystone-Ingham Corp.
13844 Struikman Road
Cerritos, California 90701

Matheson Dyes and Chemicals
Marion Place
London E81CP, England

Putnam Dyes
Quincy, Illinois 62301

Pylam Products Co.
95-10 218th. Street
Queens Village, New York 11429

Rit
Best Foods Division, CPC International
1137 W. Morris Street
Indianapolis, Indiana 46206

Screen Process Supplies Manufacturing Co.
1199 East 12 Street
Oakland, California

7 K Color Corp.
927 N. Citrus
Hollywood, California 90038

Stein, Hall and Co.
285 Madison Avenue
New York, New York 10017

Winsor and Newton Inc.
555 Winsor Drive
Secaucus, New Jersey 07094

WAXES

Alexander Sanders & Co.
Route 301
Cold Spring, New Jersey 10516

American Art Clay Co.
Rub 'N Buff Division
Box 68163
Indianapolis, Indiana 46268

Bareco Division
69 10 W. 14th Street
Tulsa, Oklahoma 74115

Binney & Smith, Inc.
380 Madison Avenue
New York, New York 10017

Lee Ward
840 N. State
Elgin, Illinois 60120

Norman Ceramics Co. Inc.
252 Mamaroneck Avenue
Mamaroneck, New York

GENERAL BATIK SUPPLIES

Aiko's Art Materials
714 N. Wabash Avenue
Chicago, Illinois 60611

Arts & Crafts Inc.
321 Park Avenue
Baltimore, Maryland

Craftool
1 Industrial Road
Woodbridge, New Jersey 07075

Crafts Unlimited
20 Macklin Street
London WC2, England

W. Cushing & Co.
North Street
Kennebunkport, Maine 04046

J.C. Larson Co., Inc.
7330 N. Clark Street
Chicago, Illinois 60626

Reeves and Sons Ltd.
Lincoln Road
Enfield, Middlesex, England
(also 108 Kensington High Street
London W8, England)

INDEX

Edited by Jennifer Place
Designed by Robert Fillie
Set in 10 point Century Expanded by Publishers Graphics, Inc.
Printed and bound by Halliday Lithograph Corp., Inc.
Color printed in Japan by Toppan Printing Company Ltd.